The Food Supply Chain in India

Analysing the Potential for International Business

About the Authors

Arpita Mukherjee is a Professor at Indian Council for Research on International Economic Relations (ICRIER), New Delhi. She has several years of experience in policy-oriented research working closely with the governments in India and the UK. She has conducted studies for various international organisations and Indian industry associations. Her research is a key contributor to India's negotiating strategies in the on-going Doha Round of WTO negotiations, in bilateral trade agreements and in domestic policy reforms. She has a PhD in Economics from the University of Portsmouth, UK. Her research interests include: services, WTO, bilateral/regional agreements; infrastructure, FDI, agriculture reforms, retail, migration and labour market programmes. She has over 80 publications including books, journals, working papers and government reports. Dr Mukherjee has presented her research at various international and national conferences.

Tanu M. Goyal is a Research Associate at ICRIER. Her research interests include trade in services, foreign direct investment issues and retail. She has over five years of research experience and has worked on projects for the Government of India, Asian Development Bank (ADB), European Commission (EC), Konrad-Adenauer-Stiftung (KAS), Italian Trade Commission, among others. She has extensively worked on international agreements and has authored reports providing negotiating strategy for the bilateral agreements being negotiated by the Indian government. She has published several international and national journal articles, book chapters, reports and other popular media articles on policy and trade issues. She has a Masters degree in Economics with specialisation in world economy, from Centre of Trade and Development (CITD), Jawaharlal Nehru University, New Delhi.

Parthapratim Pal is a faculty member in the Economics Group at the Indian Institute of Management Calcutta (IIMC). He has a PhD from Jawaharlal Nehru University in New Delhi. He has done his Masters and MPhil in Economics from the same university. He has worked in the areas of macroeconomics, development, financial markets and international economy. Before joining IIMC, Prof Pal worked with the ICRIER and the Indian Institute of Foreign Trade, New Delhi. He has published his works in various national and international books and journals. He has also worked as external consultant for organisations like TERI (The Energy and Resources Institute) and Ministry of Commerce, Government of India.

Saubhik Deb is an economist and independent consultant. He has a PhD in Economics from Rutgers University, USA and an MA and MPhil from Jawaharlal Nehru University, New Delhi. He has worked as an Economist with World Bank at Washington DC. He has also worked as external consultant for ADB and ICRIER. He is working in the areas of development economics and open-economy macroeconomics and has published his works in various national and international journals.

The Food Supply Chain in India

Analysing the Potential for International Business

Arpita Mukherjee
Tanu M. Goyal
Parthapratim Pal
Saubhik Deb

INDIAN INSTITUTE OF MANAGEMENT
CALCUTTA

ACADEMIC FOUNDATION
NEW DELHI
www.academicfoundation.com

First published in 2014
by

ACADEMIC FOUNDATION
4772-73 / 23 Bharat Ram Road, (23 Ansari Road),
Darya Ganj, New Delhi - 110 002 (India).
Phones : 23245001 / 02 / 03 / 04.
Fax : +91-11-23245005.
E-mail : books@academicfoundation.com
www.academicfoundation.com

in association with

Indian Institute of Management, Calcutta.

Disclaimer:
The findings/views/opinions expressed in this book are solely those of the authors and do not necessarily reflect the views of the publisher or the organisations they represent.

Cataloging in Publication Data–DK
Courtesy: D.K. Agencies (P) Ltd. <docinfo@dkagencies.com>

The food supply chain in India : analysing the potential for international business / Arpita Mukherjee ... [et al.].
p. cm.
Includes bibliographical references (p.).
ISBN 9789332701380

1. Food supply–India–Management. 2. Food industry and trade–India. 3. Grocery trade–India. 4. Business logistics–India. 5. India–Commerce. 6. International trade. I. Mukherjee, Arpita. II. Indian Council for Research on International Economic Relations.

DDC 338.1954 23

Typeset by Italics India, New Delhi.

Printed and bound by The Book Mint, New Delhi.
www.thebookmint.in

Contents

List of Tables, Figures and Boxes

Tables

Figures

Boxes

Abbreviations

3PL	Third-Party Logistics
4PL	Fourth-Party Logistics
AMUL	Anand Milk Union Limited
APMC	Agricultural Produce Marketing Committee
B2B	Business-to-Business
B2C	Business-to-Consumer
BIS	Bureau of Indian Standards
BMEC	Bengaluru–Mumbai Economic Corridor
BRC	British Retail Consortium
BTIA	Broad-based Trade and Investment Agreement
CAGR	Compound Annual Growth Rate
CCEA	Cabinet Committee on Economic Affairs
CONCOR	Container Corporation of India
CPC	Central Processing Centre
DIPP	Department of Industrial Policy and Promotion
DMI	Directorate of Marketing and Inspection
DMIC	Delhi–Mumbai Industrial Corridor
DTA	Domestic Tariff Area
EIC	Export Inspection Council
ESIC	Employee State Insurance Corporation
EU	European Union
FASAR	Food and Agribusiness Strategic Advisory and Research
FDI	Foreign Direct Investment
FEMA	Foreign Exchange Management Act
FICCI	Federation of Indian Chambers of Commerce and Industry
FIPB	Foreign Investment Promotion Board
FPI	Food Processing Industries
FSSA	Food Safety Standards Act
FSSAI	Food Safety and Standards Authority of India
GDP	Gross Domestic Product
GST	Goods & Services Tax
IBA	Indian Beverage Association
ICAN	Integrated Composite Application Network
ICRIER	Indian Council for Research on International Economic Relations
IMF	International Monetary Fund
IPR	Intellectual Property Rights
ITC	India Tobacco Company
JNPT	Jawaharlal Nehru Port Trust
MNCs	Multinational Corporations
MOFPI	Ministry of Food Processing Industries
MSEs	Micro and Small Enterprises
MSMEs	Micro, Small and Medium Enterprises
NABARD	National Bank for Agriculture and Rural Development
NOC	No Objection Certificate
NSDC	National Skill Development Corporation
NSSO	National Sample Survey Office
PPC	Primary Processing Centres
PPP	Public-Private Partnership
RBI	Reserve Bank of India
SEZs	Special Economic Zones
SIA	Secretariat for Industrial Assistance
SIDBI	Small Industries Development Bank of India
SMEs	Small and Medium Enterprises
TCS	Tata Consultancy Services
TRIPS	Trade-Related Aspects of Intellectual Property
UAE	United Arab Emirates
UHDP	Ultra High-Density Plantation
UK	United Kingdom
US	United States
VKGUY	Vishesh Krishi and Gram Udyog Yojana
WTO	World Trade Organization

Acknowledgements

We would like to express our deepest appreciation to all those who provided us support during this project. Foremost, we would like to thank the Foreign and Commonwealth Office (FCO) of the British High Commission, United Kingdom (UK), for sponsoring this study. We are especially grateful to Aarti Kapoor, Gaurav Gurang, Pallavi Kalita, Kiraan Sharma and Mohit Bansal for their constant support and encouragement during the project.

We want to express our gratitude to several policy makers in India and the UK who improved our understanding of the subject. In India, Siraj Hussain, Ashok Gulati, Sumanta Chaudhuri and Abhijit Sen deserve special mention. Tim Render (of the Department for Environment, Food and Rural Affairs, UK) helped to set up our meetings in London with several policy makers, covering a wide range of issues including food safety, food exports, retail regulation and consumer protection. Representatives from the delegation of the European Commission to India and from various embassies such as the United States of America and Germany helped us understand the concerns of international businesses in India. We are obliged to Jaimini Bhagwati, Former India Ambassador to the UK, for his insights and would like to thank the Indian Embassy, UK, for its help and support.

Adam Burden and his colleagues from the British Retail Consortium provided useful insights into the global retail scenario. Several Indian and foreign companies in food processing, retail and supply chain businesses participated in the survey and provided us with information on their experiences, market potential and the barriers that they face in India. Interactions with Indian chambers of commerce and industry associations deepened our knowledge of the subject. We are especially grateful to Shilpa Gupta and her team at FICCI for setting up our meetings with industry and facilitating industry interactions. We would like to thank Ajay Vir Jhakar of the Bharat Krishak Samaj for the farmers' perspective, Debraj Sengupta of the PHD Chambers of Commerce and Industry for giving us the views of small and medium enterprises and Tara Panjwani and her colleagues at the UK–India Business Council for organising an industry interaction in the UK. We would also like to thank industry experts—Arvind Singhal and Tarun Jain (Technopak Advisors Private Limited), Anil Rajpal (Tata Consultancy Services), Amit Lohani (Forum of Indian Food Importers) and Kumar Rajagopalan (Retailers Association of India)—for sharing their insights.

The authors have benefitted from discussions with Jaya Chakraborty De of Dena Bank, Aniruddha Bagchi of the Small Industries Development Bank of India (SIDBI), Manas Ranjan Mohanty, Satyajit Diwedi and S.V. Sardesai from the College of Agricultural Banking, Reserve Bank of India, B.S. Suran, P. Satish and N. Mehrotra of the National Bank for Agriculture and Rural Development (NABARD) and A. Guha and K.V. Raju of the Institute of Rural Management, Anand.

Bhavook Bhardwaj and Surbhi Sania did case studies of organised retailers, which have been used in this report. We would like to thank Renu Gupta for copyediting and Anu Mohandas for formatting the report. Sanu Kapila of Academic Foundation always responds positively to our last-minute requests for publication.

Executive Summary

India is a large emerging market with long-term growth prospects. The country has the potential to become one of the largest food-producing countries in the world. With a huge population base, India is also one of the largest food-consuming countries. The middle class population of India is larger than the population of countries such as the United Kingdom (UK) and Italy.

Food and grocery is one of the key sectors in India, which accounts for over 30 per cent of India's consumption basket. With the increase in GDP, rise in per capita income, growth of the middle class and changes in the demographic profile, there has been a change in food consumption patterns towards more processed and ready-to-eat food. The increasingly younger population has created a demand for new products, more brands and better convenience in shopping. Companies in the food business have responded positively to the changes in consumption patterns. The Indian government is encouraging investment in the food supply chain by liberalising the foreign investment policy and through subsidies and incentives. Several Indian corporate and foreign businesses have shown an interest in entering the food supply chain of India.

Given this background, this report analyses the potential for international businesses in the food supply chain of India. Specifically, the report looks at their modes of entry and operation and their contribution to the Indian economy. It examines regulations in the food supply chain in order to help international businesses understand the regulations. Based on secondary information and a primary survey, it identifies the barriers faced by international businesses and suggests a go-to-market strategy for them. It makes policy recommendations to the Indian government so that the country can attract the desired foreign investment and technology, encourage the growth of the organised sector and manufacturing, create quality employment and link Indian suppliers (farmers, manufacturers, etc.) to the global supply chains and production networks of global multinationals in the food supply chain business. The report covers retailers, manufacturers and food logistics service providers.

The report finds that there is huge untapped potential in India's food supply chain for international companies in the food business. Some of the advantages India has are its democratic set-up, varied raw material base, sound legal system and a large, skilled workforce that is available at competitive rates.

The study shows that the food supply chain faces a quasi-federal governance structure with state governments playing a key role in the regulations. At the centre, foreign direct investment (FDI) policies are currently fairly liberal and, in fact, foreign investment is encouraged in manufacturing and in food-related logistics. There are FDI restrictions in multi-brand retail and foreign retailers face discriminatory treatment *vis-à-vis* large domestic retailers. Food importers face high tariffs and quantitative restrictions on certain products. However, peak tariffs in India for agro-products are lower than in developed markets such as the EU. The Food Safety and Standards Act (FSSA), 2006, has several implementation issues that adversely affect all companies in food businesses (domestic and foreign).

The report highlights that the easiest way to enter the Indian market is through the manufacturing and test marketing routes. If a foreign company sets up a wholly-owned subsidiary in manufacturing, it is treated as an Indian company and so FDI-related restrictions in retail do not apply to them. In the fast food segment, franchising has been a successful mode of operation for foreign businesses in India. Several low-cost volume retailers have entered the market through the wholesale cash-and-carry route where 100 per cent FDI is allowed. The single-brand retail route has not been beneficial for companies in the food business. The present multi-brand retail policy is riddled with restrictions and creates an uncertain operating environment for foreign businesses. Due to higher tariffs, sporadic implementation of import restrictions and regulations such as FSSA, 2006, it is difficult to import food products into India and this difficulty is likely to continue. The non-store retail format is growing at a rapid pace; however, it has not taken off in the food and grocery segment due to regulatory and other barriers. The report found that there are huge opportunities to investment in the logistics supply chain, especially in cold chains, 3PL and 4PL systems, logistics-related IT (information technology) solutions and logistics consultancies. India is promoting the development of economic corridors and there is potential for companies to invest in this segment.

The report highlights that in an emerging market like India, which has its peculiarities, international businesses have to carefully design a go-to-market strategy. They should have a clear understanding of the regulations, identify states with conducive policies and select the right partner. Foreign companies should be aware that India is a heterogeneous market where consumption patterns differ across states and sometimes within states. They have to know their consumers and customise the products. Brand consciousness among Indian consumers is low, but price consciousness is high. There is a need for brand visibility, marketing and proper packaging and storing technologies. Sometimes, organised players have to partner with unorganised manufacturers and retailers to enhance their reach. India is a difficult market for companies in the food business and it may be difficult to reap short-term profits. A long-term phased investment plan (at least 3 to 5 years) with clear strategies will ensure success in the Indian market.

The primary survey found that India may have benefitted from the presence of foreign businesses in the food supply chain. Several foreign companies have invested in manufacturing in India, leading to employment creation. They have brought in the latest technical know-how and their global best practices. Some of the foreign firms have successfully established backward linkages and are working with farmers and contract manufacturers. These firms have contributed substantially to government revenues. Consumer awareness is rising, but they have benefitted from wider choice and better product quality. There are also some additional benefits from the presence of international businesses, such as implementation of waste management and environment-friendly technologies, product innovation and enhanced exports from India.

It is recognised that increased investment is going to play a crucial role in the development of the food supply chain in India. To supplement public investment in this sector, the government is keen to get private and foreign investment in the food supply chain. However, FDI inflows are low and the investment received by India, to date, is much below its potential. This is due to various barriers to entry and operation for foreign businesses. Specifically, the report focuses on regulatory hurdles such as the non-transparent and ambiguous FDI policy in multi-brand retail, multi-layered taxes, delays in implementing the single goods and services tax (GST), restrictions on packaging and labelling, and somewhat misleading trade and incentive policies. There are some structural issues (such as the lack of raw materials of processable quality) and procedural issues (such as delays in granting product approvals under the FSSA) that the country needs to address.

The primary survey found that when the objective of a policy is not clear, the policy becomes ineffective. This has been the case in allowing only partial FDI in multi-brand retail. Ideally, the objective of the retail policy should be to attract FDI, while the objective of retail regulation should be to ensure competition, safeguard consumer interests and create employment. India can attract FDI through a simplified retail policy that may have a sourcing clause of 30 per cent but allows foreign businesses to source from whoever they want. The policy can have a minimum investment requirement, but foreign businesses should have the flexibility to decide where they want to invest. Zoning regulations, if implemented, should apply to all large businesses and the condition that states have the right to permit or reject FDI should be reviewed and if required removed from the FDI policy. India has a low manufacturing base and a negative balance in trade in goods. The report suggests that if a foreign retailer sources more than 80 per cent of its products from India and is a net foreign exchange earner, it should be encouraged to invest by raising the FDI limit to 75 per cent. This would incentivise foreign investors to invest more and source from India. The survey found that a brand-based FDI retail policy has created ambiguity in its definition of brands, sub-brands, etc. It recommends that the government should allow FDI in multi-brand retail in a phased manner and within three years, replace it with a consolidated and simplified policy on FDI in retail, as is done globally.

The report makes several suggestions on how India can streamline the supply chain through efficient regulation and green channelling (as in the EU) and learn from global best practices. The report also emphasises inter-government collaboration and setting up joint working groups of policy makers, academics and industry from India and countries such as the UK for knowledge sharing and the development of regulations, which would benefit the country.

Introduction

India is one of the largest and fastest-growing democracies with long-term growth prospects. Globally, India is the 11th largest economy in terms of nominal gross domestic product (GDP) (US$[1] 1.85 trillion).[2] According to the International Monetary Fund (IMF), in 2010 India's GDP grew at 10.1 per cent compared with 10.4 per cent in China, 9.5 per cent among developing countries in Asia and 7.4 per cent among emerging and developing economies. Although India's growth rate slowed substantially in 2011 to 6.8 per cent, it was still higher than the average growth rate of emerging economies (6.4%) (IMF, 2012). More recently, growth has slowed further, but other fast-growing countries such as China have also seen a slowdown in growth. In 2013, the Indian economy grew at 4.4 per cent, while China's growth rate was 7.7 per cent. The Indian economy is expected to revive and is projected to grow at 6.4 per cent in 2014.[3]

With the rise in GDP and economic growth, there has been an increase in per capita income and consumption. From a per capita income of around $740 in 2005, India's per capita income more than doubled to $1,490 in 2012.[4] There has been a decline in the number of people below the poverty line, while the numbers in the middle and upper income groups have increased. Between 2001 and 2010, the size of the rich consumer class in India increased by 21.4 per cent, while the middle class grew by 12.9 per cent (Shukla, 2010), and the percentage of the deprived household class fell by 2.1 per cent. McKinsey Global Institute (2007) forecast that if the Indian economy grows at the rate of 7.3 per cent, then by 2025, 583 million Indians would join the middle class, and the share of the middle class would increase from around 5 per cent of the population in 2005 to 41 per cent in 2025. Even though in terms of percentage share in total consumer class India's middle class has a lower share (12.8%), in absolute numbers (153 million) (Shukla, 2010), it is much higher than the population of countries such as the United Kingdom (UK), Italy and Germany.[5] They would account for 59 per cent of the country's consumption by 2025. Although the growth rate has slowed, recent studies show that the Indian middle class has significant growth potential and India's consumer spending will increase (Ernst and Young, 2012).

Along with the rise in income, there have been demographic changes in the country (Sinha and Kar, 2007). More women are entering the workforce and nuclear households are replacing the joint family system. This has created a demand for convenience in shopping and packaged food. India also has one of the youngest populations in the world (54% of Indians are below the age of 25) (National Commission on Population, 2006). Young Indians aspire to better standards of living; they are more willing to try new products and are more brand and quality conscious (Mukherjee *et al.*, 2012). With higher incomes, a younger population and more women in the workforce, there is an increasing trend towards eating out and buying packaged food products. With the proliferation of media, there is greater exposure to global products and lifestyles, and with the increase in overseas travel, there is greater awareness of global shopping patterns and international brands (Rao, 2000). All these factors have led to an increased willingness to try new products and brands, which has led to the proliferation of brands and products in the processed food segment.

Food and grocery is one of the largest segments of the retail sector in India, which is changing rapidly due to the entry of domestic and foreign companies in this segment. Since the liberalisation of the economy in the 1990s, the sector has witnessed double-digit growth along with product diversification and brand proliferation to keep pace with consumer demand and preferences. The large consumer base in India has attracted several domestic and foreign companies to invest in this sector. In addition, the Indian government has undertaken several initiatives to attract investment in the food processing sector, food retail and allied logistics services.

Given this background, this report: (a) examines the opportunities and potential for international businesses in the food supply chain of India, (b) makes international businesses better acquainted with the Indian market by providing detailed information about the central and state governments policies on the food supply chain, (c) highlights the barriers faced by international businesses in India, (d) suggests a go-to-market strategy to facilitate the entry of international businesses in the Indian

---

1. Unless otherwise stated, $ will represent United States (US) dollar throughout the report.
2. *http://data.worldbank.org/indicator/NY.GDP.MKTP.CD* (last accessed on March 7, 2014).
3. IMF World Economic Outlook Update, January 2014, accessible at *http://www.imf.org/external/pubs/ft/weo/2014/update/01/pdf/0114.pdf* (last accessed on March 8, 2014).
4. *http://data.worldbank.org/indicator/NY.GDP.MKTP.CD* (last accessed on March 7, 2014).
5. *https://www.cia.gov/library/publications/the-world-factbook/geos/uk.html* (last accessed on March 10, 2014).

market, (f) identifies the current and potential gains for India from the entry of foreign businesses in the food supply chain and (g) makes policy recommendation to the Indian government based on a clear understanding of the expectations and experiences of international businesses in India, so that the country is able to attract the much-desired foreign investment and benefit from it.

This report covers food retailers, manufacturers and logistics services providers and is based on secondary information and a primary survey conducted in India and the UK.

1

Opportunity India: The Fast-Growing Food and Grocery Market

India's food demand outcomes will have a profound impact on assessment of long-term prospects of world agriculture and nutrition. India plays a pivotal role in long term projections because of its size and huge potential for increasing food demand....

Food and Agriculture Organisation of the United Nations Report on *World Agriculture Towards 2030/2050*.[1]

The Indian food industry is currently valued at ₹ 2,476.8 billion ($39.71 billion) and is expected to reach ₹ 4,080.4 billion ($65.41 billion) by 2018, registering a growth of 11 per cent.[2] Food and grocery constitute a substantial part of India's consumption basket accounting for around 31 per cent of the total consumption basket. In contrast, consumers in other countries spend a much lower proportion of their income in food and grocery—9 per cent in the United States (US), 17 per cent in Brazil and 25 per cent in China (The Boston Consulting Group, 2012).

India's retail market was valued at $490 billion in 2013 and modern retail had a share of 8 per cent of the total retail market. India's retail market is likely to grow to $865 billion by 2023 and the share of modern retail is likely to grow to 24 per cent of the total retail market (Figure 1.1).

Food and grocery is the largest segment in India's retail sector, with a share of 69 per cent in India's total retail market size in 2013.[3] India ranks third after China and the US in the top 10 global grocery retail markets.[4]

At present, the bulk of the food and grocery is in traditional corner shops also known as unorganised retail. Even though the share of modern retail or corporate retail[5] in the food and grocery retail market is only 3 per cent, it has more than doubled since 2008 and is likely to grow further.

Figure 1.1

Size and Growth Projections for the Indian Retail Sector

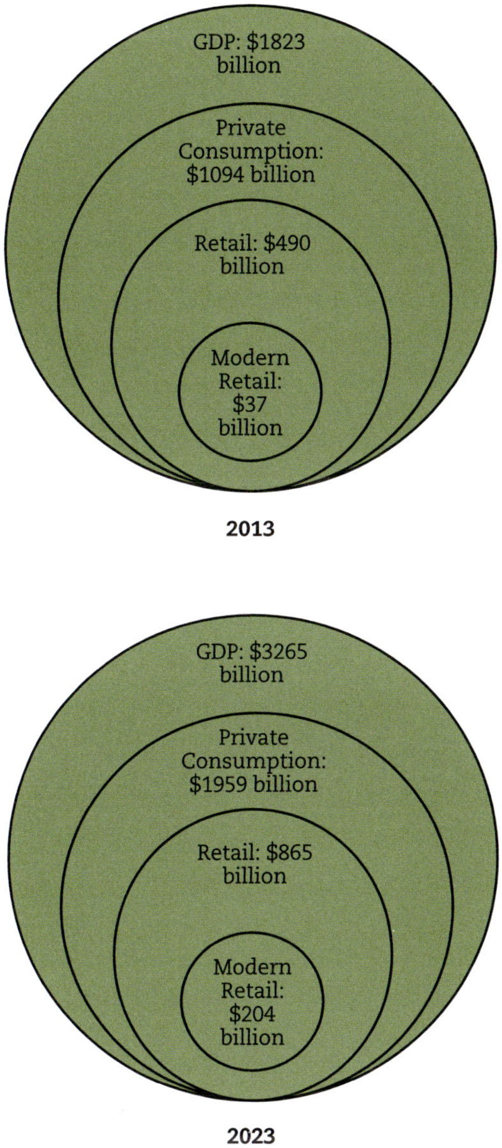

Source: Technopak Advisors Private Limited.

The growth of the modern retail sector has led to the evolution of different formats in food retail, including hypermarkets such as Auchan India and Dairy Farm Group, supermarkets such as More Megastore and neighbourhood convenience stores such as Reliance Fresh and Big Apple. According to Technopak's estimate, in 2013, there were over 280 hypermarkets and over 1,850 supermarkets that sold food and groceries.

1. *http://www.fao.org/fileadmin/templates/esa/Global_persepctives/world_ag_2030_50_2012_rev.pdf* (last accessed on March 8, 2014).
2. Indian Brand Equity Foundation.
3. Technopak Advisors Private Limited.
4. Information provided by British Retail Consortium (BRC).
5. Modern retail is defined as a type of retail that has a corporate management. Generally, these are retail chains (unlike the one-shop family-owned traditional outlets) that are professionally managed with a transparent accounting system, centralised quality control and sourcing. They are also known as organised retail.

Box 1.1

Advantage India

India has significant raw material advantages in terms of fruits, vegetables, milk, poultry and meat products. In terms of yield and output, India ranks:

- First in the world in production of guava, papayas and mangoes.
- First in the production of ginger, potatoes, garlic, dry onions, green peas, pumpkins, gourds and cauliflower.
- First in the production of pulses and chickpeas and second in rice, wheat, cashew nuts and groundnuts.
- First in the production of milk (fresh, whole, buffalo) and third in eggs.
- First in respect of buffaloes, second in cattle and goats, third in sheep and fifth in ducks and chickens.

Source: *Annual Report 2011-12*, Ministry of Animal Husbandry, Dairying and Fisheries, and *Annual Report 2012-13*, Ministry of Food Processing Industries, Government of India.

The development of modern retail has also led to the development of retail infrastructure; the number of shopping malls increased from three in 1999 to 280 in 2007 and is expected to increase at a compound annual growth rate (CAGR) of more than 18.9 per cent between 2007 and 2015 (Images, 2009). Modern retail initially started in India in large/metro cities, but is now penetrating into smaller cities where the growth rate is faster than in large cities.

While there are tremendous opportunities on the demand side, India also provides a strong supply base for companies in food businesses. India is the world's second largest producer of food after China. Its arable land area of 159.7 million hectares (394.6 million acres) is the second largest in the world (after the US).[6] India has a strong raw material base for the food processing industry (Box 1.1).

With its vast production base, India has the potential to become one of the largest food suppliers to the world and at the same time serve its own vast population.[7] Over time, there has been a continuous increase in the production of food processing industries. The total value of the Indian food processing industry is expected to touch $194 billion by 2015 from a value of $121 billion in 2012, registering a growth of around 20 per cent per annum.[8]

While India has strong demand and a raw material base, its supply chain for food businesses is still in a nascent stage. However, the food logistics/supply chain business is growing at a rapid pace and has huge untapped potential. The Indian logistics sector accounted for a turnover of $90 billion in 2011. The sector was growing at around 15 per cent per annum until the recent slowdown of 2012 (Deloitte–ICC, 2012). In general, food logistics grows at 2.5 times the growth of the economy. According to the National Sample Survey Office (NSSO), in 2011–12 the transport and storage segments[9] together contributed about 6.7 per cent to India's GDP (at factor cost and at 2004–05 prices).[10]

In India, the size of the cold storage market is around $3 billion and is growing at a CAGR of 11 per cent. The perishable product transaction value in India is estimated to be around 230 million metric tonnes. Cold storage facilities are available for only 10 per cent of this produce and of that the majority (around 90%) of the facilities are for potatoes. At present, India is able to store only 2 per cent of its farm produce in

6. *http://www.ers.usda.gov/topics/international-markets-trade/countries-regions/india/basic-information.aspx* (last accessed on March 10, 2014).
7. *Annual Report 2012-13*, Ministry of Food Processing Industries, Government of India.
8. Indian Brand Equity Foundation.
9. NSSO classifies the transport sector under the category 'transport, storage and communications,' in which 'transport' is divided in two sub-segments: 'railways' and 'transport by other means.'
10. Calculated from the Central Statistical Organisation (CSO) database, Ministry of Statistics and Programme Implementation, Government of India.

a temperature-controlled environment compared to 8 per cent in Asia-Pacific and 85 per cent in Europe and North America. This results in losses of up to 30 per cent of farm output after harvest. India requires cold storage facilities for an additional 370 million metric tonnes for perishable commodities. Thus, there is huge potential to invest in this sector (PHD Chambers of Commerce and Industry and Yes Bank Limited, 2012).

Within the transport sector, roads account for the majority (about 60–65%) of domestic freight movement, railways account for 30–33 per cent, maritime (coastal and inland) is close to 5 per cent and the remainder is through air carriers. In international trade, shipping is the dominant mode of freight transport, accounting for about 90 per cent by volume (and 70% by value). India has a long coastline of about 7,500 kilometres and has 13 major ports and 187 minor ports. Through private partnership, several airports have been developed in Delhi, Mumbai, Hyderabad and Bengaluru. The Indian government has initiated several projects to develop the railway network for dedicated freight movement between four metropolitan cities in India, namely Delhi, Mumbai, Chennai and Kolkata. The country already has a well-developed road network known as the 'Golden Quadrilateral,' which is interlinked with state highways. There is tremendous opportunity for foreign business to invest in the dedicated economic corridors and set up industrial clusters. In this context, the ongoing project of the Delhi–Mumbai Industrial Corridor (DMIC), which is supported by Japanese funding, and the Bengaluru–Mumbai Economic Corridor (BMEC), where UK companies have expressed a strong interest, deserve special mention. The Asian Development Bank has expressed an interest in investing in the Kolkata–Chennai Economic Corridor. Once there is investment in these corridors, India can develop as a production hub that is connect to global production networks.

The above discussion highlights that India is rapidly becoming an important player in the global food market due to its rising demand and supply potential. In addition to the large domestic market, India offers a large skilled workforce at competitive prices. The democratic set-up provides a stable business environment. India has a fairly strong legal system (based on British laws) and the IPR (intellectual property rights) regime is compliant with the World Trade Organization's (WTO) Trade-Related Aspects of Intellectual Property (TRIPS) agreement. All these factors have made India an attractive destination for foreign companies in food businesses. The Indian government has initiated policy measures to facilitate the entry of foreign investments in the country. The next section discusses the regulatory structure and the current regulations and incentives for investment in the food business in India.

Figure 1.2

Opportunity India

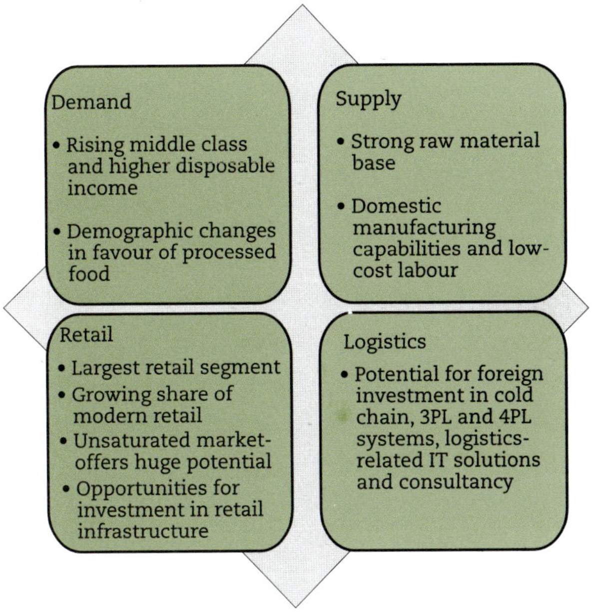

Source: Compiled from the survey.

2

Regulatory Framework and Regulation in Food Supply Chain

This section discusses the regulatory framework and regulations affecting the food supply chain business in India with a focus on regulations that impact food wholesale and retail, food imports, agro-processing and logistics. Wherever possible, we have drawn comparisons with different countries. The section is divided into three sub-sections: Section 2.1 discusses the regulatory framework, Section 2.2 examines the regulations applicable to the food supply chain and Section 2.3 highlights some government incentives for investing in the food supply chain in India.

2.1 Regulatory Framework

India has a quasi-federal governance structure with the responsibilities divided between the central, state and local governments. The responsibilities between the central government and the state governments and the areas of joint responsibility are listed in the Indian Constitution under three lists: Union List, State List and Concurrent List. Figure 2.1 shows the division of responsibility for the food supply chain.

Figure 2.2 shows the responsibilities of different ministries/departments of the central government. Agriculture and the retail sector come under the state government and the central government plays a limited role except in drawing up broad regulations for areas such as FDI in retail. The states play a significant role in decisions on product sourcing, taxes and interstate mobility of agriculture products. They also play a key role in giving licences for retail operations along with the local bodies (see Appendix A-2.1). As with retail, there is no separate ministry for the logistics sector at the centre and there are different ministries for different types of transport such as road transport, railways, shipping, ports and air transport. There is a clear division of responsibility between the central and state governments in providing transport facilities.

States with a population of over one million have local governments or municipal corporations. These are responsible for town planning and zoning.

Figure 2.1

Food Supply Chain: Division of Responsibility under the Constitution of India

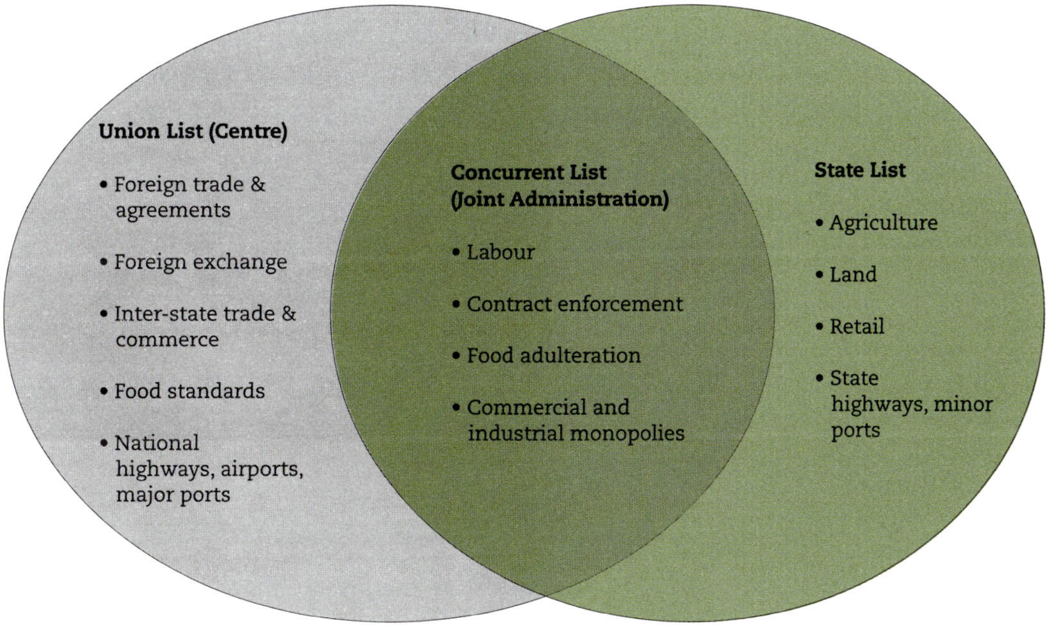

Source: Compiled from the Constitution of India, 1950.

Figure 2.2

Select Ministries that Regulate the Food Supply Chain and their Role

Ministry	Role
Ministry of Food Processing Industries (MOFPI)	Nodal ministry for food processing
Ministry of Agriculture	Nodal ministry for agricultural research, agro-food pricing and agro-development
Ministry of Health and Family Welfare • Department of Health and Family Welfare o Food Safety and Standards Authority of India	Ministry responsible for food safety regulations
Ministry of Consumer Affairs, Food and Public Distribution • Department of Consumer Affairs o Office of Legal Metrology • Department of Food and Public Distribution	Nodal ministry for consumer protection and internal trade
Ministry of Commerce and Industry • Department of Commerce (DoC) o Directorate General of Foreign Trade (DGFT) • Department of Industrial Policy and Promotion (DIPP)	Nodal ministry for external trade, export promotion and foreign investment
Ministry of Finance • Department of Economic Affair o Foreign Investment Promotion Board (FIPB) • Department of Revenue o Central and State taxes and duties	FIPB offers a single window clearance for proposals on FDI in India that are not allowed access through the automatic route. Department of Revenue is responsible for tax and duty collection of the government
Ministry of Environment and Forests	Environmental clearances for manufacturing
Ministry of Micro, Small and Medium Enterprises (MSME)	Issues related to MSMEs in India including collaborations and schemes
Planning Commission	Five year planning and budget allocation
Competition Commission of India (CCI)	Regulates anti-competitive practices
Ministry of Labour and Employment	Central government labour regulations
Ministry of Rural Development	Land reforms and other matters like administration of Land Acquisition Act
Ministry of Urban Development	Monitors the programmes on urban development in the country
Reserve Bank of India	Central bank and manager of foreign exchange

Source: Compiled from different websites of the Government of India.

2.2 Regulations Affecting Food Businesses

Multiple regulatory bodies at the central, state and local levels have led to multiple regulations in the food supply chain business in India. The regulations are either: (a) enacted by the central government and have to be mandatorily implemented by the centre and the states, (b) enacted by the central government and can be voluntarily implemented by the states, (c) enacted by the states and implemented by them and (d) enacted by the states and implemented by local bodies. At the centre, there are some regulations such as allowing FDI in retail that can be implemented by the Cabinet (constituting a set of key ministers), while other regulations such as changes in the Foreign Exchange Management Act (FEMA), 1999, need the approval of Parliament. Most regulations apply to both domestic and international food businesses and are non-discriminatory for foreign service providers. However, in some areas, there are restrictions that apply only to foreign companies.

2.2.1 FDI Regulations and Restrictions

FDI regulations in India are generally imposed and implemented by the central government.[1] A foreign investor in India falls under the FEMA, 1999,[2] of the Ministry of Finance. The Act is managed by the

1. The only exception to this is the multi-brand retail FDI policy where implementation is at the state level.
2. *http://finmin.nic.in/the_ministry/dept_eco_affairs/capital_market_div/FEMA_act_1999.pdf* (accessed on February 12, 2014).

Reserve Bank of India (RBI), the central bank, and it consolidates and amends laws related to foreign investments in the country and profit repatriation.[3]

Foreign investment regulations are issued by the Department of Industrial Policy and Promotion (DIPP). In India, FDI is allowed through two routes: (a) automatic route and (b) government route. Under the automatic route, no prior approval of the government is required, while under the government route, proposals for FDI have to be cleared by the Foreign Investment Promotion Board (FIPB), constituted by the Ministry of Finance. The FIPB is an inter-ministerial body that examines and discusses proposals for foreign investments in select sectors. The Minister of Finance considers the recommendations of the FIPB on proposals for foreign investment up to ₹ 12 billion ($193.5 million).[4] Proposals involving foreign investment of more than ₹ 12 billion ($193.5 million) require the approval of the Cabinet Committee on Economic Affairs (CCEA).

Over time, the FDI policy in India has been liberalised. From an economy that was closed to foreign investments until 1991, India now allows FDI in almost all sectors except sectors such as insurance, postal services, gambling and retail where there are complete or partial FDI restrictions.[5]

The FDI regulations across different sub-sectors are discussed below.

2.2.1.1 Food Processing/Manufacturing

The Indian government encourages foreign investment in manufacturing in the food processing sector and there is no discrimination between foreign and domestic investment in this sector. FDI up to 100 per cent through the automatic route is allowed for all processed food products except for items reserved for micro and small enterprises (MSEs), which include pickles, chutney and bread, among others. For manufacture of items reserved for MSEs, FDI is permissible under the automatic route up to 24 per cent. If the foreign investment is more than 24 per cent, it requires FIPB approval. Such an undertaking requires an industrial licence under the Industries (Development & Regulation) Act, 1951.[6]

2.2.1.2 Supply Chain

Foreign investment is encouraged in supply chain and 100 per cent FDI is allowed under the automatic route in storage and warehousing, which includes warehousing of agricultural products with refrigeration or cold chains. FDI up to 100 per cent is also allowed in IT (information technology) software related to supply chain development, trucking services, etc. The government has allowed foreign investment in dedicated freight corridors such as the Bangalore–Mumbai Economic Corridor (BMEC). However, there are FDI restrictions in certain segments of logistics such as air transport (FDI up to 49 per cent is allowed in scheduled air transport and 74 per cent in non-scheduled air transport).

2.2.1.3 Distribution and Retail

- 100 per cent FDI is allowed in the wholesale cash-and-carry[7] segment through the automatic route. It is subject to the condition that wholesale trade to group companies taken together should not exceed 25 per cent of the total turnover of the wholesale venture. In addition, a wholesale trader cannot open a retail outlet and sell directly to consumers.

- 100 per cent FDI is allowed in test marketing under the government/FIPB route. In August 2013, the Indian government changed the conditions for FDI in test marketing. Previously, investment in test marketing was only allowed for items for which the retailer had approval for manufacturing and the manufacturing facility needed to be set up simultaneously with the commencement of test marketing for the product. Moreover, test marketing was only allowed for a period of two years. In the renewed policy,

3. At present, necessary changes in the FEMA regulation to allow FDI in multi-brand retail are under review with Parliament.
4. Conversions are made using the RBI exchange rate on February 17, 2014: $1 = ₹ 62.27.
5. For details, see the DIPP Consolidated FDI Policy, October 2013, accessible at *http://dipp.nic.in/English/Policies/FDI_Circular_01_2013.pdf* (accessed on January 8, 2014).
6. Ministry of Food Processing Industries.
7. In India, wholesale trade is defined as sale of goods/merchandise to retailers, industrial, commercial, institutional or other professional business users or to other wholesalers and related subordinated service providers. Wholesale trading would, accordingly, be sales for the purpose of trade, business and profession, as opposed to sales for the purpose of personal consumption. The yardstick to determine whether the sale is wholesale or not would be the type of customers to whom the sale is made and not the size and volume of sales. Wholesale trading would include resale, processing and thereafter sale, bulk imports with export/ex-bonded warehouse business sales and B2B e-Commerce.

the government has withdrawn all these conditions.[8]

- 100 per cent FDI is allowed in single-brand retail and 51 per cent FDI in multi-brand retail, subject to certain conditions. From August 2013, the entry routes for FDI in single-brand retail have been modified. Previously, FIPB approval was required for 100 per cent investment, but now up to 49 per cent investment is allowed under the automatic route; only investments exceeding 49 per cent require FIPB approval.
- In September 2012, the Indian Cabinet allowed 51 per cent FDI in multi-brand retail, subject to certain conditions, which was cleared by Parliament in December 2012. These conditions were further explained and to certain extent modified in August 2013 through DIPP Press Notes 5 and 6 (see Appendix A-2.2 for details on the single-brand and multi-brand FDI policy).
- For e-commerce activities, 100 per cent FDI is permitted in B2B through the automatic route; however, FDI is prohibited in B2C operations.

A foreign retailer can operate in India through the wholesale cash-and-carry route, franchising (allowed through RBI approval on a case-by-case basis), distribution and commission agents, single-brand retail and partial FDI in multi-brand retail. The FDI policy imposes certain conditions that discriminate against foreign retailers *vis-à-vis* domestic retailers. Specifically, in the case of multi-brand retail, there is a minimum capital requirement, a mandatory condition of 30 per cent local sourcing, state governments have the right to not allow FDI and foreign retailers are not allowed to do e-tailing.

2.2.2 Regulations Affecting the Food Supply Chain

Regulations affecting different segments of the food supply chain are given in Appendix A-2.3. The regulations affecting food imports, retail operations, consumer protection and anti-competitive practices are discussed as follows.

8. 'Consolidated FDI Policy (effective from April 5, 2013)', DIPP, Ministry of Commerce and Industry, Government of India, and Press Note 6, DIPP, Ministry of Commerce and Industry, Government of India.

2.2.3 Regulations affecting Food Import

The import of food products is governed by multiple regulations in India. These include the Food Safety and Standards Act (FSSA), 2006 (Ministry of Health and Family Welfare), Legal Metrology Act, 2009 (Ministry of Consumer Affairs), Livestock Importation Act, 1898 (Ministry of Agriculture) and Plant Quarantine Order, 2003 (Ministry of Agriculture).

2.2.3.1 Food Safety and Standards Act, 2006

In August 2011, India implemented the FSSA, 2006, and the implementation of this Act is compulsory in every Indian state. This Act led to the establishment of the Food Safety and Standards Authority of India (FSSAI), which lays down safety and quality standards for food items and regulates their manufacture, storage, distribution, sale and import. This Act applies to all in the supply chain, except the farmers. The Act has consolidated several central acts and orders that applied to the food sector, with the objective of effective implementation, transparency and accountability. The previous acts and orders included the Prevention of Food Adulteration Act, 1954; Fruit Product Order, 1955; Solvent Extracted Oil, De-Oiled Meal and Edible Flour (Control) Order, 1967; Meat Food Products Order, 1973; Edible Oils Packing, 1998; Vegetable Oil Products Order, 1988; and Milk and Milk Product Amendment Regulations, 2009.

The FSSA has six key regulations related to food import business:

- Licensing and Registration of Food Businesses Regulation.
- Packaging and Labelling Regulation.
- Food Product Standards and Food Additives Regulation.
- Prohibition and Restriction on Sales Regulation.
- Contaminants, Toxins and Residues Regulation.
- Laboratory and Sampling Analysis Regulation.

All food business operators in India, whether domestic or foreign, require an FSSAI licence to conduct business in the country. Globally, countries have the right to set their own standards and definitions. The Indian FSSA 2006 is different from the European Union (EU) food safety regulations and standards. For instance, in India, a product label has to carry the name and address of the manufacturer and the importer, while the EU requires information on the manufacturer or the packager or the seller. In India, product labelling can be in English or Hindi; in the EU, member states have different language requirements. Overall, the food safety standards are based on the Codex Alimentarius and in 2013, the FSSAI began to harmonise its regulations with Codex Alimentarius. This process is still underway.

2.2.3.2 Legal Metrology Act, 2009

The Legal Metrology Act, 2009, establishes uniform standards of weights and measures. According to the Legal Metrology Packaged Commodities Rules, 2011 (which came into force on April 1, 2011), manufacturing, packing, selling or importing any pre-packaged commodity is prohibited unless it is in a standard quantity and carries all prescribed declarations. The Legal Metrology Act, 2009, imposes standard pack sizes for certain commodities as a consumer protection measure. This Act requires that the maximum retail price should be mentioned on the product label, which is not required by the EU.

2.2.3.3 Livestock Importation Act, 1898

This Act regulates, restricts or prohibits the import of any livestock that may affect human or animal health.

2.2.3.4 Plant Quarantine Order, 2003

This is an order by the central government to prohibit and regulate the import of agricultural goods.

2.2.3.5 Other Standards and Labelling Requirement

Import of products such as milk-based products, baby food and food additives have to comply with Indian quality standards and importers have to register with the Bureau of Indian Standards (BIS). BIS is under the Ministry of Consumer Affairs, Food & Public Distribution. These standards are also applicable to domestic businesses.

The Export Inspection Council (EIC) along with the Ministry of Commerce and Industries has laid down guidelines, acts and regulations on imported commodities. These are based on international standards—Codex Alimentarius. The EIC monitors imports of food items and checks the condition of the hold in which the goods are being transported, the visual/physical appearance of the goods and the labelling of the products. Customs officials check the consignments of edible/food products imported through ports, inland container depots, air cargo complexes, container freight stations and land customs stations. The port health officer checks the samples of imported food products. In addition, every imported food item at the time of its import is examined to have a valid shelf life of not less than 60 per cent of its original shelf life;[9] food articles that do not meet this condition cannot be sold in the domestic market. The Ministry also imposes labelling requirements such as the requirement to print information on the month and year when the commodity was manufactured/packed or imported.

2.2.3.6 Import Tariffs

In India, tariffs are used as a tool to protect the domestic industry and as a source of revenue for the Ministry of Finance. India has imposed high tariffs on most agricultural commodities. However, the peak tariff in India is lower than in several countries, including the EU (Table 2.1).

India also imposes import restrictions/quotas/ quantitative restrictions on products such as sugar and cotton yarns. In the WTO, India has a defensive position in agriculture negotiations and is a proponent for safeguards and special and differential treatment on the grounds that the agriculture sector in India is highly fragmented with small and marginal landholdings.

2.2.4 *Regulations on Retail Operations*

Retailers in India are regulated by multiple authorities and regulations (see Appendix A-2.1 for the list of licensing bodies). These are largely at the state and local levels. In India, a retailer has to obtain more than 50 licences issued by multiple authorities. These include a Shops and Establishment Trade Licence, police clearance, FSSAI licence and fire clearance, among others. These are similar to retail regulations in developed countries such as the UK where a retailer has to get licences from more than 60 authorities such as Department of Transport, Department of Health and Fire Officer. However, there are key differences in the retail regulations of India and countries such as the UK. First, unlike the UK, domestic large retailers in India do not face any

9. *http://www.sethassociates.com/food-and-drug-industry-in-india.html* (last accessed in June 2013).

discriminatory treatment *vis-à-vis* traditional, small and family-owned businesses. In most countries, including a number of the EU Member States, zoning regulations are applicable to all large retailers, which restricts them from locating in certain parts of the cities, but such restrictions are either not there or not strictly implemented in India. This is due to the lack of proper urban planning. In India, foreign retailers face additional restrictions and requirements (including zoning regulations) as stated in the FDI policy.

2.2.5 Regulations for Consumer Protection

The Consumer Protection Act, 1986, and the Consumer Protection (Amendment) Act, 2002, by the Ministry of Consumer Affairs provide guidelines for the protection of consumer interests and rights in India. These Acts also make provisions for the establishment of consumer councils and similar authorities to settle consumer grievances and disputes. The Indian consumer protection regulation is outdated and does not cover issues such as a cooling-off period, which is crucial in the case of sale through non-store formats such as direct selling. The government is in the process of designing a new regulation.

2.2.6 Regulations to Check Anti-competitive Practices

Earlier, the Monopolistic Restrictive Trade Practices Act, 1969, regulated issues related to competition. This Act was substantially taken from UK legislations, particularly the Restrictive Trade Practices Act, 1956, and the Resale Prices Act, 1964. The main functions of the Act were to ensure that the operation of the economic system did not result in the concentration of economic power in the hands of a few, to provide for the control of monopolies and to prohibit monopolistic and restrictive trade practices. With economic development, reforms and liberalisation, the Act underwent revisions. In 2002, Parliament enacted the Competition Act, 2002, and it was amended in 2007. The central government also established the Competition Commission of India to prevent practices that have an adverse effect on competition. The Indian regulation is modelled on the EU anti-competitive regulations. The Competition Act, 2002, covers issues such as predatory pricing. However, unlike countries such as the UK, which has a Groceries Code Adjudicator for anti-competitive practices by large grocery retailers, India is yet to have a retail-specific anti-competitive regulation.

2.3 Incentives for Investment in the Food Supply Chain

Since food processing is a priority sector for the Indian government, it offers several incentives and schemes to attract investments. States such as Andhra Pradesh, Bihar and West Bengal have a

Table 2.1

Applied MFN Tariff Rates of India and EU by Product Group

Products	*Average Applied MFN Rate*		*Percentage of Duty-free Tariff Lines*		*Maximum Applied MFN Tariff*	
	India (2010)	*EU-27 (2011)*	*India (2010)*	*EU-27 (2011)*	*India (2010)*	*EU-27 (2011)*
Dairy products	33.7	55.2	0	0	60	205
Fruit, vegetables, plants	30.3	11.5	1.3	18.8	100	170
Coffee, tea	56.1	6.2	0	27.1	100	25
Cereals & preparations	30.7	16.3	11.9	12.0	150	167
Oilseeds, fats & oils	18.8	7.1	16.9	43.5	100	171
Sugars and confectionery	34.4	29.1	0	0	60	131
Beverages & tobacco	70.8	19.2	0	19.8	150	162
Other agricultural products	21.5	4.8	11.2	65.1	70	131
Textiles	13.3	6.6	0	2.1	106	12
Clothing	15.1	11.5	0	0	315	12

Source: Compiled from WTO (2012).

Figure 2.3

Schemes for Food Supply Chain

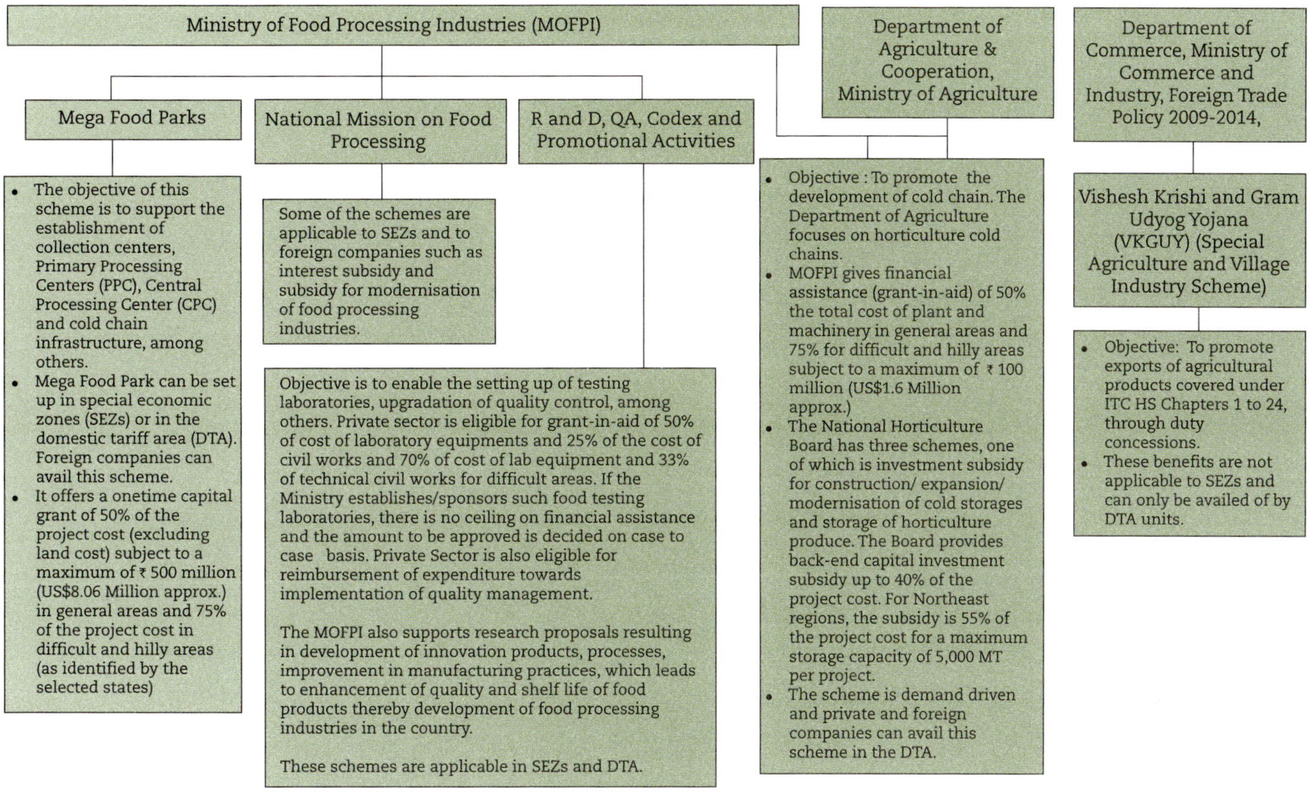

Source: Compiled from the websites of the Ministry of Food Processing Industries, Ministry of Agriculture (Department of Agriculture & Co-operation), and Ministry of Commerce and Industry, Government of India.

dedicated policy for the food processing industry.[10] Different ministries including the Ministry of Agriculture, the Ministry of Food Processing Industries and the Ministry of Commerce have their respective schemes and incentives. Most of the schemes are targeted at investment in small and medium enterprises and some of the schemes are available to both domestic and international businesses. Some of these incentives are linked to exports and the establishment of special economic zones (SEZs) for exports, while others are targeted at both exports and the domestic market. These are compiled in Figure 2.3.

10. For details, see *http://www.investindia.gov.in/?q=node/64* (accessed on February 13, 2014).

3

Presence and Experiences of Select Global Players in the Food Supply Chain

The large Indian market has attracted foreign businesses to the country. However, after its independence in 1947, India adopted an inward-looking import substitution policy, which led to FDI restrictions, high tariffs and quantitative restrictions on imports. Some companies such as the Coca Cola Company had to exit from India due to restrictive regulations that adversely impacted their operations. In the mid-1980s, India started the liberalisation process and in 1989, the multinational company PepsiCo Inc. entered the Indian market. Major reforms took place in the early 1990s when the country faced a severe balance of payments crisis. The reforms were undertaken in a phased manner and they covered the liberalisation of foreign investments in manufacturing, removal of the licensing raj, removal of quantitative restrictions on imports and reductions in tariffs, among others. Today India's autonomous liberalisation is much higher than its commitments in the Uruguay Round of the WTO. Foreign investors and companies have responded positively to the liberalisation process. In the 1990s and the 2000s, several global manufacturers and logistics companies entered the Indian market. Several global manufacturers used the merger and acquisition route and the contract manufacturing model to gain a foothold in the market. Since the year 2000, global retailers have shown a keen interest in the Indian market. Even in sectors such as retail, where there are FDI restrictions, foreign retailers have entered and are operating in various formats such as franchising and wholesale cash-and-carry. Thus, the policy of not allowing FDI in retail is not an entry ban. It only restricts foreign retailers in selecting their preferred entry route. Some of the experiences of foreign companies in the food supply chain are discussed below.

3.1 Wholly-owned Subsidiary in the Manufacturing Sector

In India, 100 per cent foreign-owned subsidiaries are allowed in manufacturing (including the food processing sector). Foreign companies that are incorporated under the Indian Companies Act (1956 and 2013) as Indian private limited companies enjoy the same treatment as Indian companies and are allowed to retail their brands in the Indian market without any restrictions. Several multinationals in food businesses have wholly-owned subsidiaries in manufacturing; examples are ITC Limited, Hindustan Unilever Limited and PepsiCo India. These companies get the same treatment as domestic companies and they do not face the barriers to retail faced by companies that want to enter through the retail route. ITC's experience in India is discussed in Box 3.1.

Box 3.1

ITC Limited: Long-standing Presence in India

Established in 1910, for the first six decades ITC was involved in manufacturing cigarettes and in the packaging and printing business. After operating in several verticals such as the hotel and hospitality industry, in 1990 ITC set up the Agri Business Division for export of agri-commodities. The division is one of India's largest exporters. In 2001, ITC entered the food business with the introduction of ready-to-eat Indian dishes. ITC introduced several food brands such as Aashirvaad, Candyman and Sunfeast that have become a part of the Indian food basket. These brands are sold by both large and small retailers in the country and are rapidly penetrating the country. To suit the needs of Indian customers, ITC started several initiatives such as mobile vending stores in Hyderabad in which it gives refrigerated pushcarts to street vendors who go from door-to-door to sell fresh produce. It also started an e-choupal initiative in which ITC used information technology to provide useful information to farmers in India. E-choupal also linked rural farmers to procurement centres *via* the Internet. ITC has ventured into the lifestyle retail segment and has recently started selling specialised food and grocery products through its lifestyle retail outlets. The FMCG segment of ITC was valued at ₹ 70 billion ($1.1 billion)* in 2012-13 and is likely to grow to ₹ 150 billion ($2.4 billion) in 2017-18. The company is now expanding its presence to other markets such as Nepal and is also constantly enlarging its footprint in India.

Note: * Conversions are made using the RBI exchange rate on February 17, 2014. $1 = ₹ 62.27

Source: Company website accessible at *http://www.itcportal.com/about-itc/profile/index.aspx* and *http://www.thehindu.com/business/Industry/itc-to-double-sales-of-noncigarette-fmcg-biz/article5135176.ece* (last accessed on February 25, 2014).

Box 3.2

Metro Cash-and-Carry: India Operations

The first Metro Cash & Carry centre in India opened in Bangalore in 2003 and at present there are 15 wholesale centres, including two in Bangalore, Hyderabad and Mumbai, one each in Jaipur, Ludhiana, Jalandhar, Amritsar, Delhi, Kolkata, Vijayawada, Indore and Zirakpur. Metro Cash & Carry started its presence in bigger cities; however, given the Indian market, Metro opened smaller stores in Tier 2 and 3 cities, as these are not mature markets. The stores stock only a few categories of products. Metro Cash & Carry sources 95 per cent of its products locally. In India it has joined hands with various government agencies; it has an agreement with the Punjab Agro Industries Corporation and it has set up agriculture sourcing platforms—'farmer's collection centres' in Karnataka, Andhra Pradesh, Punjab, Maharashtra and West Bengal. Metro has its own distribution channel and logistics solution in India. Due to its B2B operating model, Metro is doing well even in states such as West Bengal where the state government is opposed to FDI in retail. In West Bengal, small retailers are the largest buyers from Metro Cash & Carry stores. According to an estimate, in 2012 Metro generated revenue of 355 million ($492 million)* from India, which is around one per cent of the company's global revenue.

Note: *Converted using *www.oanda.com* with an exchange rate of 1 = $1.38 as on March 12, 2014.

Source: *http://www.metro.co.in/public/home; http://www.smartinvestor.in/market/Compnews-206578-Compnewsdet-Metro_Cash_amp_Carry_revamps_India_strategy.htm; http://www.indexmundi.com/g/r.aspx?v=67;* (last accessed on February 24, 2014).

3.2 Franchising[1]

This is a popular route for foreign retailers in India. There are no specific regulations governing franchisee operations in India; however, international businesses entering through this route do fall under the FEMA Act, 1999, the India Contract Act, 1972, competition laws, intellectual property laws and consumer protection laws. Most companies in the fast food business including McDonald's, Subway and Baskin Robbins have entered the Indian market and expanded their operations in the country through this route. McDonald's has been growing at 30–40 per cent since 2000. It started operations in India in 1996 with two outlets: one in Delhi and one in Mumbai. It is now present in 40 cities and has around 250 outlets across the country. It has successfully set up a pan-India supply chain and has four distribution centres to cover these 250 outlets (for details, see Sharma, 2013). McDonald's has customised its products to suit the tastes of Indian consumers—the *McAloo Tikki* burger caters to the large vegetarian population and beef and ham products have been removed from its menus to address religious sensitivities. These are examples of how companies reorient their products to suit local taste patterns. Within a span of less than 10 years, Subway has established a presence in 50 Indian cities and serves over 15,000 customers per day.[2] Among foreign retailers, Group Auchan SA, a French multi-brand retailer, established a presence in India through a franchise agreement with Max Hypermarket India Private Limited of the Landmark Group. It has 13 hypermarkets operating in India as of February 2014.[3]

3.3 Wholesale Trade/Cash-and-Carry Operations

Foreign companies such as Metro Cash & Carry GmbH (Germany), Carrefour S.A. (France), Tesco PLC (UK) and Wal-Mart Stores Inc. (US) entered through this route. The experience of Metro Cash & Carry in India is discussed in Box 3.2. Different businesses adopted different models to enter through this route. For instance, while Tesco PLC and Wal-Mart entered India through a joint venture with an Indian partner, Carrefour and Metro established a 100 per cent subsidiary. Tesco PLC chose the Tata Group, and Wal-Mart decided to form a partnership with Bharti Enterprise. Both Tata Group and Bharti Enterprise are large Indian conglomerates with a pan-India

1. While Indian law does not define franchising, the term indicates a way of doing business that involves the use of a person (franchisee), pursuant to a licence, of another person's (franchisor's) business model, name, image and business identity along with know-how to exploit his intangible assets in a particular territory for a specified period, with or without assured financial returns to the franchisor. For details, see KPMG (2013).

2. *http://businesstoday.intoday.in/story/subway-restaurant-increase-outlets-india-by-2015/1/24516.html* (last accessed on February 25, 2014).

3. See *http://www.auchanindia.com/about.html* (accessed on February 19, 2014).

presence, but the Tata Group has ventured into retail while Bharti Enterprise is a telecommunications company. Tesco has continued its partnership with the Tata Group in the retail segment, but Wal-Mart diluted its partnership with Bharti and now operates as a 100 per cent subsidiary in the wholesale cash-and-carry business.

3.4 Single-brand Retail Trade

Foreign retailers have not used the single-brand route to enter the Indian market in the food and grocery segment. The survey found that Marks & Spencer India, which has approval for single-brand retail, considered bringing its food and grocery products to India through the single-brand retail route, but the proposal was not approved.

3.5 Multi-brand Retail Trade

The majority of foreign food and grocery retailers are multi-brand retailers. For a long time, FDI in multi-brand retail was not allowed. As a result, most foreign multi-brand retailers entered the Indian market through the wholesale trading route. The government allowed FDI in multi-brand retail trade in September 2012, subject to certain conditions that were considered restrictive by foreign retailers. As a result, no foreign retailers entered India through this route, and subsequently in August 2013, the government made changes and brought more clarification into the policy. Following this, Tesco PLC applied for entry through the multi-brand retail route and announced that it would first establish a retail presence in the states of Maharashtra and Karnataka. In December 2013, the Foreign Investment Promotion Board (FIPB) cleared the Tesco PLC application for a $110 million FDI inflow. The survey found that the company is satisfied with the August 2013 notification. However, after the FIPB approved Tesco PLC's proposal, the state governments of Delhi and Rajasthan rolled back the policy of allowing FDI in retail. Since Maharashtra will also hold elections in 2014, this has created an uncertain operating environment for Tesco PLC and other multi-brand retailers that have plans to enter India. It is expected that foreign retailers such as Tesco PLC will move cautiously until the policy stabilises and others will closely watch Tesco PLC's experience before deciding on their entry strategy.

3.6 Sourcing from India

Indian food products and spices (for example, *tikka masala*) have a distinct market in foreign countries. It was pointed out during the survey that there is a huge Indian diaspora that ensures constant demand for Indian products. Products such as Indian spices, tea and basmati rice are procured directly by foreign retailers or channelled through Indian exporters and distributors. Some foreign companies have acquired Indian companies or work directly with contract manufacturers to source products from the Indian market. For instance, the British beer manufacturing company, Cobra Beer, has acquired breweries in Bihar. Foreign retailers such as Waitrose (UK) and Aldi Einkauf GmbH (Germany) retail products such as Assam Tea and Basmati rice in countries, some of which are sourced from India. Waitrose's sister organisation, John Lewis Partnership, has a sourcing office in India and they source some ingredients and products such as curry paste from the Indian market. Other companies like J Sainsbury Plc have recently opened a sourcing office in India, which is being used to source non-food products. The majority of retailers establish a sourcing or buying office in India before their entry into retail.

3.7 Exporting Products to India

Several foreign companies want to export food products to India to cater to the large market. These are either procured directly by large Indian retailers or are sold through Indian distributors and importers. For instance, Waitrose has entered into an exclusive agreement with HyperCity Retail India Limited of the Raheja Group (a large Indian multi-brand retail chain) to export and sell Waitrose brands in India through their retail outlets. Waitrose exports products to more than 50 countries and want to do the same in India.

Indian importers such as Max Foods Private Limited import products and brands such as Walkers (Scotland), Campina (UK), Kraft Foods (UK) and Doritos (US). These importers work with multiple suppliers, exporters and manufacturers in different countries.

Several companies, after importing products into India, started manufacturing them locally as they realised the market potential. For instance, Cadbury, which is a British multinational confectionery company owned by Mondelēz International, started its operations in India by importing products into the country. As the market for its products grew, it established a manufacturing presence in India as a wholly-owned subsidiary of the Mondelēz International Group. The company introduced products such as Oreo biscuits and Toblerone in India and after these products percolated in the market, the company has now entered into local manufacturing. Ferrero Rocher, a product of Ferrero International, was also imported into India and is now manufactured in India.

3.8 Non-store Retail Formats

Foreign investment in e-retail is prohibited but several Indian companies have venture capital funding for e-retail. E-retail has seen double-digit growth in India. In the case of direct selling, there is ambiguity in the FDI policy and most direct selling companies have entered India through the test marketing and/or the manufacturing route. Globally, Amway Inc., Herbalife International and others sell food supplements and nutritionals through the direct selling route. In India, some of them sell health and wellness products.

3.9 Logistics and Food Supply Chain

Only a few foreign companies operate in the logistics segment of the food supply chain as the supply chain infrastructure in India is still underdeveloped and companies have to make very large investments to set up end-to-end food supply chains. One of the largest foreign companies that provides complete logistics solutions in India is Maersk India Private Limited, which is a wholly owned subsidiary of the Denmark-based Maersk Group. It is a key partner of Indian exporters for products such as banana (see Box 3.3).

Maersk India Private Limited has also invested in setting up logistics infrastructure in India. It formed a joint venture with the Container Corporation of India (Concor) to set up a cargo terminal at Nhava Sheva port in Mumbai.

While Maersk India Private Limited provides complete logistics solutions, other companies such as Danfoss (a Danish company) provide specialised services such as cold storage facilities. In India, Danfoss is incorporated at a wholly owned subsidiary of the Danfoss Group. Snowman Logistics Limited, which is a joint venture between Gateway Distriparks Limited, Mitsubishi Corporation and Nichirei Corporation of Japan and International Finance Corporation in India, is one of the first and the largest cold chain and logistics firm in India with pan-India operations. It provides services to several retailers (Reardon and Minten, 2011).

Foreign governments and funding agencies have partnered with the Indian government and private players to build infrastructure and freight corridors. For instance, the India–Japan partnership in developing the Delhi–Mumbai Freight Corridor and the interest of the UK government and companies in developing the Bengaluru–Mumbai Economic Corridor (BMEC) have led to investments in freight corridors.

Overall, the discussion in this section highlights that foreign companies are present in different segments of the food supply chain in India. They have adopted unique business models, customised their products and changed their strategies from time to time. The interest in the Indian market is largely due to the large and growing number of upper- and middle-class consumers and the availability of a low-priced, skilled workforce. Several retailers from EU countries and other developed countries such as the US are facing a saturated domestic market, while the Indian market is unsaturated and the food supply chain has seen double-digit growth in the past decade. Many companies treat India as an alternative market to China, which enables them to diversify their risks. The next section discusses barriers in the food supply chain.

Box 3.3

Maersk India Private Limited: The Indian Banana Travels with Maersk

The Indian banana industry is highly fragmented, with marginal farms that have small landholdings. Indian exporters work with these contract farmers to enhance the yield and quality of their products. Maersk partners with Indian exporters to set up an efficient supply chain that ensures minimum wastage in transportation. Maersk helps create an unbroken cold chain from the origin to the packing house and this has reduced post-harvest waste levels during transportation to 1–2 per cent compared to 20-30 per cent earlier, representing a significant productivity gain (Figure 3.1). The company has a temperature-controlled distribution system that increases the potential travel time for bananas. This has also helped increase the export potential for bananas.

Figure 3.1

Journey of the Indian Banana

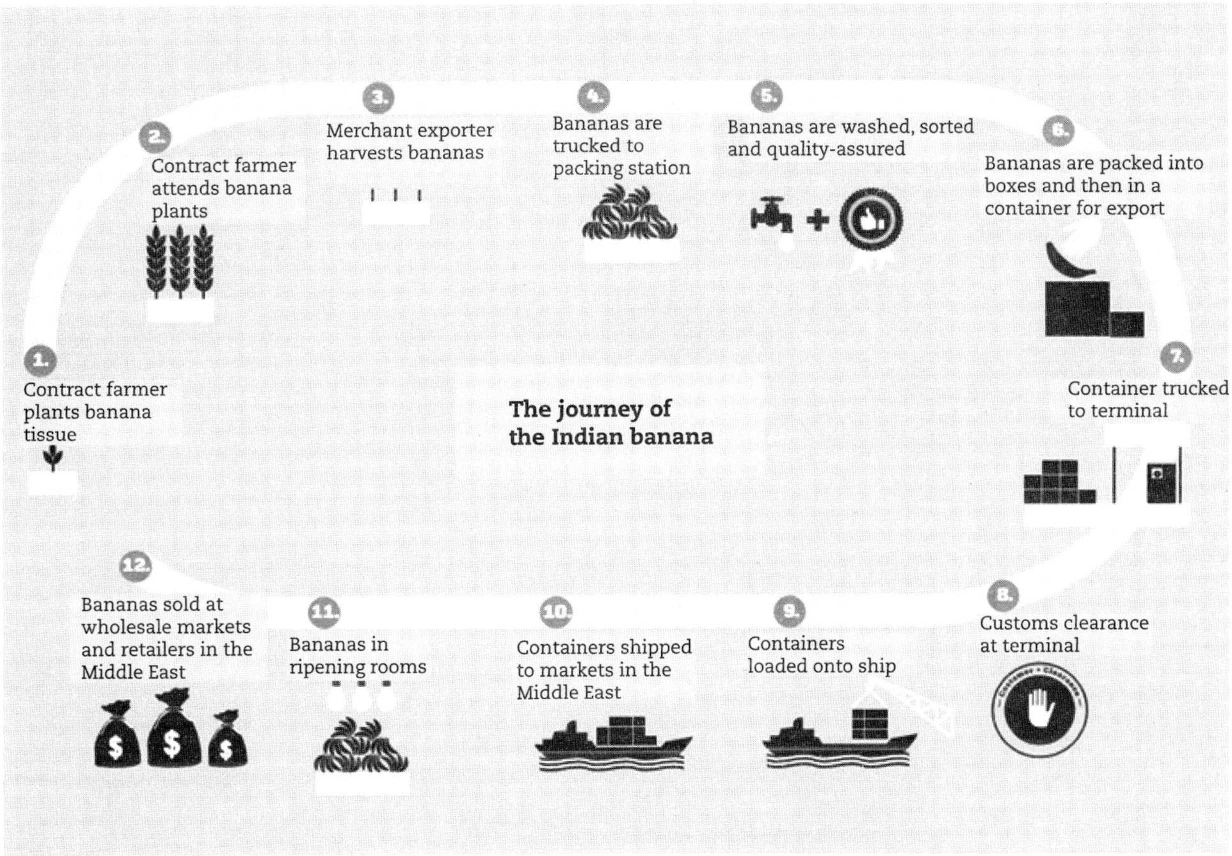

Source: Extracted from *Building Tomorrow's Markets: India's Banana Case Study – Unblocking the Potential of Indian Banana Trade*, a report by Maersk Line. Accessible at *http://www.fao.org/fsnforum/cfs-hlpe/sites/cfs-hlpe/files/files/Food_losses_waste/India%20banana%20case_final.pdf* (last accessed on February 25, 2014).

4

Barriers in the Food Supply Chain

The barriers in the food supply chain include general macroeconomic barriers and issues that are specific to companies operating in different segments of the food supply chain. The majority of the barriers are common to both Indian and foreign companies. In this section, the macroeconomic issues are discussed briefly followed by a detailed analysis of barriers specific to different players (such as manufacturers, importers and retailers) in the food supply chain.

4.1 Macroeconomic Issues

India's growth rate has slowed in the past few years. According to the International Monetary Fund's (IMF's) World Economic Outlook Update, in 2010 India's GDP grew at 10.3 per cent,[1] but the growth rate fell to 4.6 in 2013–14 and it is projected to be 5.4 per cent in 2014–15.[2] An economic slowdown adversely impacts consumer demand and purchasing power. The cost of doing business in the country is high due to infrastructure problems and regulatory hurdles. According to the World Bank's *Ease of Doing Business Index*, India was ranked 134 in 2014 among 189 countries, which is below other emerging markets such as China (96) and Brazil (116).[3]

The lack of quality infrastructure is a major barrier in India. The erratic power supply and the high cost of power have adversely impacted all types of businesses. It is difficult to get land for projects such as mega food parks and the cost of land is high (Mukherjee *et al.*, 2013). The poor quality of roads and lack of connectivity of rural roads with state and national highways is a major barrier for sourcing agriculture products. Even the speed on national highways connecting major metro cities is low. Survey participations pointed out that on average it takes almost seven days to transport food products from Mumbai to Kolkata, which is a distance of about 1,987 kilometres. The delays and lack of computerisation at check-posts along with the need for informal payments increase transit time and logistics costs. This also affects the quality of the raw materials and food products, which are perishable. The dedicated freight corridor projects are progressing at a slow pace and the Indian Railways charges a high freight rate to cross-subsidise the low passenger fares.[4]

In the past few years, India has been facing high food inflation. Average food inflation, which was only 3.8 per cent between 2007 and 2008, increased to an average yearly inflation of 10.1 per cent between 2011–12 (Gulati and Saini, 2013). The high food prices have increased the cost of raw materials for manufacturers, while consumers have to reduce their discretionary consumption.

Although India is a large market, Indian consumers are price sensitive and not very brand conscious (Mukherjee *et al.*, 2012). They have distinct food preferences that differ from global tastes. The consumers are heterogeneous and their demands for food items vary across different states of India. The consumption of packaged food and drink is lower in India than in developed countries and other developing countries. For example, per capita consumption of fruit juices in India is only 0.02 litres compared with China that has attained a level of 1.5 litres,[5] and per capita consumption of packaged drinking water in India is only 16.2 litres compared with 250 litres in Mexico.[6]

4.2 Barriers Specific to the Food Supply Chain

This sub-section focuses on regulatory barriers in the food supply chain. Then it discusses fiscal barriers, import-related barriers and other barriers.

4.2.1 Regulatory Barriers

The Indian food supply chain is governed by multiple regulatory bodies at the central, state and local levels, which has resulted in multiple regulations. Survey participants said that although in many countries the food supply chain is highly regulated, in India the central government has a limited role in regulating the food supply chain. Moreover, there is a lack of coordination between central government policies and the policies of different state governments. The

1. IMF World Economic Outlook Update, January 2011, accessible at *http://www.imf.org/external/pubs/ft/weo/2011/update/01/pdf/0111.pdf* (accessed on February 26, 2014).
2. IMF India 2014 Article IV Consultation, accessible at *http://www.imf.org/external/pubs/ft/scr/2014/cr1457.pdf* (last accessed on February 26, 2014).
3. World Bank Doing Business Report 2014, accessible at *http://www.doingbusiness.org/~/media/GIAWB/Doing%20Business/Documents/Annual-Reports/English/DB14-Full-Report.pdf* (last accessed on February 26, 2014).
4. Passenger fare-to-freight ratio in India stood at 0.25:1 in 2010-11. That is far below the corresponding average of 1.4:1 for Korea, 1.3:1 for France, 1.2:1 for China, 0.9:1 for Malaysia and Indonesia, and 0.7:1 for Thailand (Source: "Milking Freight to please Passengers", *Business Line*, February 25, 2011).
5. *http://mofpi.nic.in/ContentPage.aspx?CategoryId=547* (last accessed in May 2013).
6. *http://articles.economictimes.indiatimes.com/2012-07-03/news/32524033_1_bottled-water-water-market-capita-consumption* (last accessed in May 2013).

impact of the regulation on stakeholders depends on their involvement in the food supply chain. Some regulatory restrictions such as restrictions on FDI in multi-brand retail largely impact foreign retailers, while others such as restrictions on sourcing impact both Indian and foreign manufacturers, retailers and logistics service providers.

4.2.1.1 Restrictions on FDI in Retail

Survey participants said that India is the only country that has a brand-based FDI retail policy and the policy is unclear about how brands and sub-brands should be defined. Due to this lack of clarity, sometimes retailers are not allowed to offer the whole range of products and services. The decision to allow entry depends on the interpretation of the application by the approving agencies. For example, IKEA faced problems in getting approvals for having a restaurant in its stores. Similarly, Marks & Spencer did not get approval for food product retail when it applied through the single-brand retail route.

The retail policy is not clear with respect to the definition of store and non-store retail formats. For example, direct selling is covered under wholesale trade, while it is *sui generic* and encompasses both wholesale and retail trade (Mukherjee *et al.*, 2010). Moreover, certain non-store formats such as e-retail are prohibited under the present FDI policy.

The objective of the FDI in retail policy is not clear. While the government wants FDI in retail, it seems to impose conditions that make the policy unattractive to foreign retailers. The government aims to reach certain goals such as reduction in food inflation by allowing FDI in retail, which is difficult to achieve. Food inflation in India is mainly due to supply-side constraints, and foreign retailers can only help to streamline the supply chain if they have the supporting policies and there is an adequate supply of raw materials and food products. On January 7, 2014, the Department of Industrial Policy and Promotion (DIPP) came up with a discussion paper on e-commerce titled, 'Discussion Paper on E-Commerce in India.'[7] The paper is a collation of information on e-commerce rather than a policy guideline. During the survey, Indian industry associations pointed out that the DIPP is not clear about its objectives in the discussion paper. If the policy is to have a proper e-commerce regulation, the paper should focus on the key elements of the regulation.

The policy of allowing FDI in retail has been changed several times, which has created an uncertain operating environment. Even when the central government liberalised the FDI policy, it imposed additional requirements. For example, when the FDI limit in single-brand retail was increased from 51 per cent to 100 per cent, mandatory local sourcing conditions (sourcing from small and medium enterprises (SMEs) of a specific size) were imposed. Although the retail FDI policy can be decided by the Indian Cabinet and does not need the approval of Parliament or of the state governments, the policy was debated in Parliament. Political parties have different views on the subject; however, they have not maintained a principled stand on the matter, and change their views on retail liberalisation depending on whether they are in power or in the opposition. Retail has been a key component of the political manifestos and agendas of the major political parties during both central and state government elections. The efficacy of the retail policy has been further complicated by the requirement for state-level approvals, since retail comes under state jurisdiction. Thus, a commitment by the central government to liberalise the sector does not automatically grant foreign companies the right to have a pan-India presence in retail through the FDI route. More recently, two states—Delhi and Rajasthan—decided to roll back on allowing FDI in retail. India is holding its general elections in the year 2014 and the new government could change the FDI policy again. This has adversely affected companies such as Tesco PLC, which has made an investment commitment.

With respect to the August 2013 policy, foreign retailers pointed out that the mandatory requirement to invest in back-end operations is difficult for retailers who only deal with front-end retail and use the services of 3PL and 4PL logistics companies for the back-end. The retailers also had concerns regarding sourcing conditions from the SMEs. Sometimes SMEs do not meet the quality standards. This is especially a concern for specialised and high-end food and beverage retailers. It was also pointed out that the actual sourcing requirement depends on the consumption pattern of the target population and the 30 per cent sourcing requirement would be difficult to meet if the consumption behaviour is tilted towards products from multinational corporations (MNCs).

The government is yet to change the Foreign Exchange Management Act (FEMA) regulations to allow FDI in multi-brand retail and, hence, retailers

7. *http://dipp.nic.in/English/Discuss_paper/Discussion_paper_ecommerce_07012014.pdf* (last accessed on February 7, 2014).

may face problems in repatriating profits. Moreover, it is not easy to find a like-minded local partner in India.

4.2.1.2 Issues related to Food Safety and Standards Regulations

Packaging and labelling requirements for processed foods and beverages are governed by several regulations including the Food Safety Standards Act (FSSA), 2006, Legal Metrology Act, 2009, and standards set by Bureau of Indian Standards (BIS). Some of the regulations are evolving and are being implemented unevenly across different ports in the country. For example, in the second half of 2013, the FSSA, 2006 was stringently imposed in Nhava Sheva port in Mumbai, which led to the withholding of several consignments of imported food products due to non-conformity with Indian regulations; at the same time, consignments into Chennai port did not face this problem. Retailers and importers in India face a challenge, since they need to repackage the products to meet the Indian standards. Previously, companies were allowed to do the packaging and labelling in bonded warehouses in India; however, now they are required to pack and label the goods abroad. The government has imposed restrictions on the use of stickers on the labels. Since the Indian market for imported products is still small, it is difficult for companies, especially foreign SMEs, to design labels only for India.

There are other issues related to the existing regulations. Under the Legal Metrology (Packaged Commodities) Rules, 2011, food and beverages can only be sold in certain standard sizes that have to be printed on the package in specific units. For instance, while previously companies that produced powder for beverages could print 'number of glasses' to denote the quantity of beverage, under the new act, they need to specify the quantity in grams. Companies observed that converting 'number of glasses' to grams might result in odd package sizes that would affect their promotional activities. The rule also does not account for shrinkages in the weight of food and beverage products due to weather conditions. If the weight is found to be below the printed weight, the company is held responsible.

The FSSA, 2006, lacks supply chain traceability. It does not cover farmers and, therefore, does not cover inspection/regulation of products that are supplied by farmers. Hence, other stakeholders in the supply chain can be held responsible for adulteration due to the presence of insecticides or pesticides at the farm level. Second, the classification and categorisation of food and beverages in India differ from global categorisation. This creates problems of parity and definitional synergy for global companies, especially those involved in imports of food and beverages. The additive approval process is also not aligned at the global level. International companies pointed out that as per Schedule 4 of FSSA, 2006, separate licences are required for the manufacture and distribution of different categories of foods and beverages, including proprietary foods, genetically modified foods, health supplements, functional foods and special dietary foods. Moreover, separate licences are required from the state and central governments, which complicates the licence application and approval process.

The product approval process under the FSSA, 2006, is slow for several reasons. As per the FSSA, testing of all foods and beverages should be done in accredited laboratories. However, most states do not have adequate funds to set up a laboratory and the central government has not permitted any additional budget to the states for this purpose. There is also a lack of qualified food inspectors. Initially the Act mandated that food inspectors have a background in nutrition and food, but the lack of qualified people and pressure from trade unions led to a change in the requirement, making recruitment more flexible and allowing the recruitment of food inspectors from other science streams (such as physics). The lack of knowledge and experience of the inspectors has created problems. Overall, product approvals can take as long as nine months, which delays the establishment of manufacturing facilities.

4.2.1.3 Regulations that impact the Setting up of Supply Chains

The Agricultural Produce Marketing Committee Act (APMC, reformed in 2008) and the Essential Commodities Act,[8] 1955, adversely impact sourcing of raw materials as well as finished products. The APMC Act has not been reformed in several states and, therefore, agriculture products have to be sourced from state-controlled *mandis*. Most *mandis* suffer from poor storage, lack handling and processing facilities, and do not have marketing channels. Around 15–25 per cent of the total produce sold *via* the APMC route gets wasted due to multiple intermediaries and poor *mandi* infrastructure. Moreover, an agricultural

8. This Act provides for control over production, supply and distribution, and trade and commerce of certain commodities such as foodstuff.

commodity moving from one state to another attracts a tax or '*mandi* fee' every time it enters a new regulated market. Therefore, the cost at which the produce is available to the manufacturer rises by almost 60-70 per cent (Pachouri, 2013). Even in states where direct procurement is allowed, private players have to pay *mandi* cess. In states such as West Bengal, contract farming is not allowed and companies have to enter into agreements such as a partnership agreement with farmers for direct sourcing. The Essential Commodities Act, 1955, regulates and controls the production, distribution and pricing of certain commodities such as sugar and private players find it difficult to source such products.

4.2.2 Fiscal Barriers

4.2.2.1 Taxes

The food sector in India faces high and multilayered taxes that vary across states. This makes it difficult to have a uniform pan-India price. Certain products such as whisky, wines and spirits are heavily taxed by the central and state governments.

In addition to taxes, some states and even local bodies impose *cess* such as the Octroi in Maharashtra and the Way Bill in West Bengal. Taxes vary by product categories and processed food often faces a higher tax than non-processed food. The Indian government has proposed a single Goods and Services Tax (GST) to streamline the tax system. However, the implementation of GST is getting delayed and there are questions about whether agriculture products will be covered under GST.

4.2.2.2 Incentives

Income tax holidays and other incentives provided by the government for investment in food processing and the logistics sector (such as cold chain) are directed towards SMEs and they do not promote economies of scale. Sometimes, they are wrongly designed and, therefore, ineffective. For instance, companies involved in processing, preserving and packaging fruits and beverages get 100 per cent tax exemption on profits in the first five years of the start of business.[9] However, due to the long gestation period, companies may not be able to accrue profit in the first five years.

9. *http://mofpi.nic.in/images/File/TaxRelief_FPISector_140213.pdf* (last accessed in June 2013).

4.2.3 Trade-related Barriers

Apart from the restrictions that importers face due to regulations, high import tariffs on agro-products and delays in getting clearances from customs and other authorities are major barriers for importers. In India, tariffs on agriculture products are high, primarily to protect domestic producers and farmers. India has a defensive position in reducing agricultural tariffs even under bilateral trade agreements and this has been a key issue under the ongoing India–EU Broad-based Trade and Investment Agreement (BTIA). Interestingly, the tariff peaks are higher in the EU than in India (see Table 2.1 in Chapter 2), but while the EU is pushing for liberalisation of products in its trade agreements, India is against it. As of date, India has kept several agricultural products including whisky, wines and spirits, wheat, maize and dairy products (including milk, milk powder, ghee, butter and whey) in the sensitive/negative/exclusion list under major trade agreements. India has a large negative trade balance and there is a strong domestic lobby against tariff reduction. For example, Indian companies such as Amul (Anand Milk Union Limited) have argued that since India cannot match the high amount of subsidies given by the EU to the dairy industry, India should not open up the dairy market under the BTIA. India also uses quantitative restrictions or quotas for agricultural raw materials such as sugar, dairy products, fruits and vegetables. This implies that only certain quantities of imports are allowed at certain tariff rates.

After the implementation of the FSSA, 2006, the customs clearance process has become extremely cumbersome and causes delays. Port clearance takes almost 14 days compared with countries such as Singapore where it takes only 24 hours.

4.2.4 Other Barriers

There are several other barriers in the food supply chain. These include inconsistency in the supply and quality of raw material and the underdeveloped food processing sector. India lacks agricultural raw materials of processable quality (Mukherjee *et al.*, 2013). Due to difficulties in getting the raw materials locally, India is a net importer of processed food (also see Joshi, 2009). Only 7 per cent of the total Indian perishable produce is processed, which is extremely low compared to countries such as the US (65%), Philippines (78%) and China (23%).[10] A large part

10. Inputs from the Associated Chambers of Commerce and Industry of India (ASSOCHAM).

of the produce (almost 30% of farm produce after harvest) is wasted in the supply chain due to delays, improper handling and lack of cold storage facilities (ASSOCHAM and Yes Bank, 2012). Other problems include the high cost of production due to lack of adequate working capital and lack of technology for processing and packaging, among others.

Despite these barriers, given that India has the advantage of a large and growing consumer base and is an attractive investment destination for foreign investors, the next section discusses the go-to-market strategy for foreign players in the food supply chain, which will enable them to have successful business operations in India.

5

Go-to-market Strategy for International Businesses

The previous sections show that India is a large market where food and grocery accounts for a substantial part of the consumption basket. The food business in India has witnessed double-digit growth and is growing at a rapid pace. The market is unsaturated and there is huge potential for investment in the food supply chain. The government wants foreign investment in manufacturing and logistics services. It has allowed foreign investment in retail, subject to certain conditions, and is contemplating further liberalisation of FDI in the retail policy. Several companies have established a presence in India and are expanding at a rapid pace. Some of them face several barriers in India. A foreign company entering the Indian market has to understand the specialities of the market and then implement an India-specific go-to-market strategy. This section highlights some strategies to help companies operate successfully in India.

5.1 Identify the Right Government Agency and State

A large part of the policy with respect to the food supply chain is either enacted or implemented at the state level. Therefore, it is important for companies to identify a state government that is receptive to foreign investment. This can be difficult for manufacturers in the food processing sector who prefer to be located near the source of their raw materials. Agricultural raw materials are available in more than one state and, therefore, the company should carefully choose the ideal state for establishing operations. While it is important to have a good relationship with state governments, it is better not to be too politically inclined. In fact, a company that wants to establish a presence in India should get in touch with the Ministry of Food Processing Industry at the centre and the relevant ministries/departments of the state government. The State Industrial Development Corporations have been proactive in attracting investments; they have access to land and can help with other resources and clearances. To facilitate investment, the Indian government has set up 'Invest India,' which is a joint venture between a premier Indian chamber of commerce, the Federation of Indian Chambers of Commerce and Industry (FICCI, 51% equity), Department of Industrial Policy and Promotion (DIPP) (35% equity) and state governments (0.5% each).

5.2 Understand the Regulations

Several regulations impact the food supply chain at the central, state and local levels, and foreign companies should understand these regulations. The recent problems that food importers faced in India show that they have not understood the regulations on labelling. If they had, they would have raised an objection when the regulation was designed and inputs were sought from industry. Moreover, there are ways to circumvent the regulation. For example, if products are repackaged in India, companies can meet the Food Safety Standards Act (FSSA), 2006 regulations and other packaging and labelling regulations. It is important to note that states differ widely in their norms and regulations. For example, for environment clearance, Gujarat, Karnataka and Haryana have categorised beverages under the 'red' category along with highly polluting industries, while states such as Orissa and Himachal Pradesh have placed it under the 'orange' category. It is important for foreign companies to identify the right legal firm and the right local partner that can help them understand the regulations.

5.3 Select the Right Mode of Entry

Since India is a difficult market, a joint venture with a like-minded local partner can ease the entry process and enable the company to understand the market. Most foreign companies are not aware of the test marketing route. This is one of the most flexible routes to enter the Indian market. The most difficult route to enter the food retail business (apart from fast food chains) is the single-brand retail route. Companies that have both manufacturing and retail operations should ideally enter through the manufacturing route. This will help them circumvent the barriers related to FDI in retail. India does not encourage the import of food products. Therefore, companies are likely to face barriers in food imports. Imported products are priced high and, therefore, their market reach is limited. Unless it a specialised product such as Scotch Whisky, it is better to manufacture at least some products in India, which will enable the company to avail of the benefits. For such companies, instead of entering through the multi-brand retail route, they should enter through the manufacturing route, which will treat them the same as domestic companies. While there is a minimum investment requirement in the multi-brand retail route as well as other conditions, there are no requirements in manufacturing.

5.4 Know Your Consumers

Indian consumers are heterogeneous and their tastes and preferences vary across states and even within states (Mukherjee *et al.*, 2012). For example, while tea is preferred in north India, there is a higher preference for coffee in southern states such as Tamil Nadu. Foreign manufacturers and retailers, therefore, should have a clear knowledge about their customers' tastes, religious taboos and shopping habits, among others. Several fast food chains (including McDonald's and KFC) had to change their products to cater to local tastes. PepsiCo India launched products such as 'Nimbooz' (an Indian-style lime-based drink) and 'Kurkure' (spicy cheese puffs) for the Indian market. Once the products are successfully launched in India, many of them are exported. For example, 'Kurkure' is now available in Pakistan, Kenya and Canada. During the survey, low-cost volume retailers pointed out that they have to source around 75–80 per cent of the products locally to cater to local tastes. The demand for imported products is growing but imported products are expensive and beyond the reach of the majority of shoppers.

Indian consumers are price-sensitive and, therefore, foreign companies have adopted smart pricing strategies. For example, the Coca-Cola India launched 'Chhota Coke,' a 200 ml bottle at the price of ₹ 5 ($0.08)[1] especially for Indian consumers. This helped the company penetrate the market at a rapid pace. Until recently, companies tried different packaging sizes to penetrate the market, but the government has imposed restrictions on package sizes.

Indians prefer to shop frequently for food and groceries and they have limited refrigeration facilities. Hence, manufacturers have to ensure that the products reach the neighbourhood *kirana* stores or traditional retail outlets on time; they are also struggling to meet the price that local shopkeepers offer. Although demand for packaged food is growing, most consumers still prefer to cook at home. Indian consumers are not very brand conscious particularly for food products and they experiment with brands.

5.5 Enhance the Product and Brand Visibility through Proper Marketing

It is important for foreign companies to enhance their product and brand visibility through proper marketing. Some companies have roped in film personalities for advertisements, while others have designed innovative advertisements. Most retailers use promotions and offers by clubbing products or selling below the maximum retail price to attract consumers. While retailers prefer to use pamphlets and advertise through newspapers and the print media, large manufacturers have used television channels. Some of them also promote events such as cricket or other popular games.

5.6 Need for Proper Packaging

India has a variety of climate conditions and the storage facilities are poor and inadequate. Therefore, proper packaging is important. Several global multinationals with high quality standards have faced issues such as insects being detected inside the packages due to poor storage and packaging. Even if these problems are caused by mishandling at the retail end, manufacturers are often held responsible.

5.7 Significant Competition from *Kirana* Stores

In the food and grocery segment, local *kirana* stores have significant advantages over organised retailers and offer stiff competition. They offer services such as delivery on credit, which is difficult for organised retailers to offer. Many organised retailers now take orders on the phone and offer free home delivery, imitating the *kirana* model.

5.8 Should not Expect Short-term Profits

India is a large but a difficult market for players in the food supply chain. Companies should not expect short-term profits. The survey showed that profits can be reaped only after 3–5 years, and sometimes longer. Companies have to prepare for contingencies and delays. They should set up the supply chain and distribution network before starting operations.

5.9 Other Strategies

There are tremendous possibilities for developing logistics facilities along the economic corridors such as the Delhi–Mumbai Industrial Corridor (DMIC) and the Bengaluru–Mumbai Economic Corridor (BMEC). India is in the process of implementing GST and, if that is done, it will lead to market integration. Logistics companies have to plan for opportunities that will result from the implementation of GST. In logistics, several companies have a wholly-owned subsidiary but they generally expand through strategic alliances and partnerships. Using the

1. Conversions are made using the RBI exchange rate on February 17, 2014: $1 = ₹ 62.27.

existing network in many cases helps to reduce costs. India lacks the latest technology and there is scope for companies to enter this segment. In manufacturing, contract manufacturing is a well-established model in India and has been very successful. It also reduces costs.

6

Current and Potential Gains for India from the Entry of International Business in the Food Supply Chain

The current and potential gains for India from the entry and presence of international businesses in the food supply chain have been well documented (Annamalai and Rao, 2003; Kaur, 2013; Reardon and Minten, 2011; Sharma, 2013). Studies have shown that international businesses can provide several benefits to developing countries like India, which need technical know-how, global best practices and finance to support their growth process. These benefits range from inflow of foreign capital, employment generation, development of the organised manufacturing and services sectors, enhanced productivity and returns in the agriculture sector, enhanced tax contribution, creation of infrastructure and improved product quality and choice for consumers, among others. This section highlights some of the current and potential benefits of international businesses to the Indian economy based on a survey and published data.

6.1 Foreign Investments Inflows

In emerging markets such as India, foreign investments play a key role not only in correcting the balance of payments (BoP) situation, but also in bringing much-needed capital to finance its development process. India has a high fiscal deficit and the government is not able to invest in food supply chain infrastructure (Mukherjee *et al.*, 2013). Foreign investment can complement domestic private investment and government investment in the food supply chain.

Over the years, India has progressively liberalised the FDI regime to attract foreign investments. As a result of opening up, foreign exchange reserves in India increased from $1.2 billion in June 1991[1] to around $315 billion in December 2013.[2] While some sectors such as the manufacturing and food processing industries (FPI) have been completely opened up for foreign investment, others like retail are undergoing phased liberalisation. The food processing industry is the 12th largest foreign exchange earner in India. From April 2000 until December 2013, cumulative FDI inflow into the sector was $5.2 billion, which accounted for 2.5 per cent of the total FDI received by India during this period.[3] The year-on-year FDI inflow in food processing industries in the past five years is given in Figure 6.1.

Figure 6.1 shows that since 2000–01, FPI have been attracting foreign investments. Even during the slowdown in western markets, the sector continued to receive investments. Some of the large multinationals have announced significant future investments in India (Box 6.1).

From April 2000 until December 2013, trading services (comprising wholesale trade and other distribution services) received foreign investments worth $4.3 billion with a share of around 2 per cent in India's total foreign investment inflows. It is the 13th largest recipient of foreign investment in the country. Metro AG, a German retail and wholesale group that entered India in 2003, has invested up to ₹ 15 billion ($242 million).[4] For each of its stores in India, the company has made an investment of up to ₹ 600–700 million ($9.6–11 million).[5] It plans to open 8–10 stores in the country every year for the next four years (starting in 2014) at an investment of around ₹ 24 billion ($387 million).[6]

Compared to food processing and trading, foreign investment in retail is low. This is primarily due to FDI restrictions in the retail sector. The country started easing retail FDI restrictions from 2006, after which there have been some investments in the single-brand retail sector. However, this investment hardly covers the food retail business. Foreign investments in the single-brand retail sector amounted to $97.60 million between April 2000 and December 2013. In terms of share, retail received only 0.05 per cent of the total FDI into the country. Moreover, DIPP data shows that the trend in FDI approvals in single-brand retail has been volatile and is linked to the FDI policy in India (Figure 6.2)

Until March 2014, only one company —Tesco Plc — had applied to make investments in the multi-brand retail sector. In December 2013, Tesco Plc's $110 million investment plan was approved by the Indian

1. Montek Singh Ahluwalia's speech in the Planning Commission. Accessible at *http://www.planningcommission.gov.in/hindi/aboutus/speech/spemsa/msa012.pdf* (accessed on January 8, 2013).
2. This is the cumulative FDI inflow from April 2000 to December 2013. For details, see *http://dipp.nic.in/English/Publications/FDI_Statistics/2013/india_FDI_December2013.pdf* (accessed on March 3, 2014).
3. *http://dipp.nic.in/English/Publications/FDI_Statistics/2013/india_FDI_December2013.pdf* (accessed on March 3, 2014).
4. Conversion made using RBI exchange rate as on March 3, 2014 of $1 = ₹ 62. This also holds for the conversion in Box 6.1.
5. *http://www.business-standard.com/article/companies/metro-cash-carry-revamps-india-strategy-113102400942_1.html* (last accessed on March 3, 2014).
6. Conversion made using RBI exchange rate of $1 = ₹ 62, as on March 4, 2014.

Figure 6.1

Year-on-Year Foreign Investment Inflows in FPI since Year 2000–01 (in US$ million)

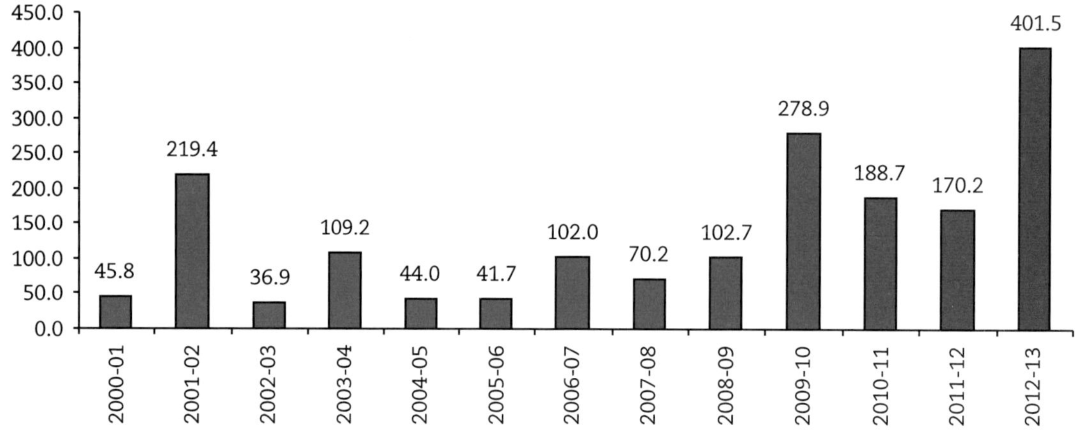

Source: Ministry of Food Processing Industries.

Figure 6.2

Trends in Approved FDI in Single-Brand Retail (Cumulative in US$ million and Percentage Share)

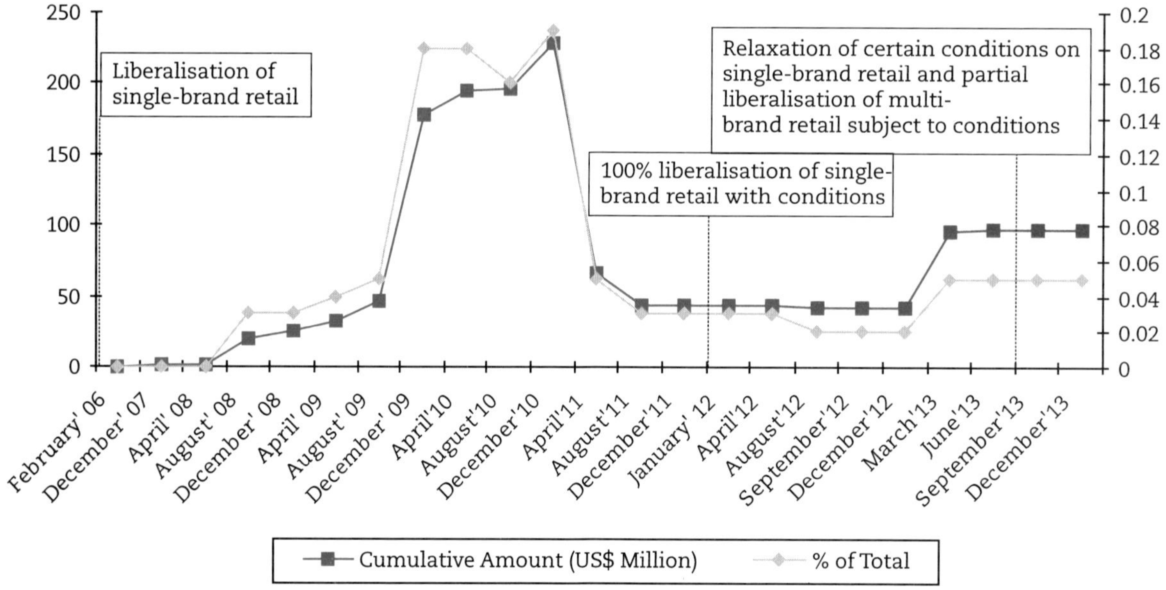

Source: DIPP FDI Factsheet, various issues.

Box 6.1

PepsiCo Inc.'s Investment in India

PepsiCo Inc., a US-based global food and beverage company, is a large investor in the Indian market. Since its entry in 1989, the company has invested around $2 billion in the Indian market, which includes investment in manufacturing and processing, agriculture, innovation and infrastructure development. Between 2008 and 2010, the company made investments of $500 million (each year) to sustain its growth in the Indian market. Until 2020, the company had investment plans of around ₹ 330 billion ($45.3 billion), of which it is planning to invest ₹ 12 billion ($193 million) in setting up a manufacturing facility in Sri City in Andhra Pradesh. This will be a greenfield investment.

Source: Primary survey

government. Other multi-brand retailers such as Carrefour S.A. have expressed an interest in entering India through the multi-brand retail route, while Wal-Mart Inc. has expressed reservations about some of the conditions in the existing multi-brand retail policy. Thus, there is interest among foreign retailers, especially low-cost volume retailers that operate in the multi-product segment, to enter through the multi-brand retail route, but they are waiting for more clarity on the policy. The ability of the country to attract future FDI will depend on the FDI policy.

6.2 Contribution to the Exchequer

International food businesses can benefit the Indian economy through their contribution to both direct and indirect taxes. Any business entity in India that has a corporate management (known as the organised sector) has to pay sales tax, value added tax (VAT), service tax and corporate tax, among others. All these taxes contribute to the revenue collection of the Indian government. A study shows that McDonald's in north India contributes around $7 million per annum as sales tax to different state governments in states where it has operations.[7] The entry of international businesses increases the share of corporate sectors in manufacturing, logistics and retail. The corporate sector contributes significantly to tax revenue. In 2012–13, the share of the corporate sector was around 43 per cent of total tax receipts, which was much higher than its share in 2005–06 of around 28 per cent.[8] In India, food processing and the food retail sector are largely non-corporate and, hence, their contribution to government revenue is limited. If the Indian economy grows and if corporate food businesses continue to grow, the government's tax collection is likely to increase.

6.3 Contribution to Employment and Skill Development

It is difficult to measure the impact of the entry of international businesses on employment in sectors such as retail and food logistics where there is a large unorganised sector with no official record of employment. The existing survey-based studies conducted for the Government of India (see Mukherjee and Patel, 2005) shows that international businesses can create additional employment opportunities in sectors such as retail if the Indian economy is growing (which implies that there is opportunity for both organised and unorganised retailers to grow, although their growth rates may vary). International businesses create employment opportunities across the supply chain. A recent study shows that in the non-alcoholic beverage sector an organised manufacturer creates 1:4 employment, that is, for each direct employment in the manufacturing sector, there are four indirect employment opportunities in the food supply chain (Mukherjee *et al.*, 2013). Direct employment includes employment created in manufacturing units, retail outlets and supply chain companies, while indirect employment includes employment generated through outsourcing manufacturing, supply chain solutions, etc. According to a report by the National Skill Development Corporation (NSDC)[9] employment in the logistics sector is likely to grow. For instance, the employment in the port sector in 2008 was 93,000 persons and it is likely to increase to about 220,000 persons by 2022. A survey-based study found that in the case of Carrefour, one store of 50,000–60,000 sq ft sales area provide avenues for approximately 200 people for direct employment and 250 people for indirect employment, which is only an estimate of the employment created in the front-end store and not the entire supply chain. Carrefour plans to provide direct and indirect employment opportunities to approximately 20,000 people in the stores by 2020.[10] Metro Wholesale Cash & Carry employs 3,119 people (as of December 2012).[11] A McDonald's restaurant in India requires around 100 people in different positions including managers, counter staff and cleaners.[12] International food businesses also create self-employment opportunities by enabling people to undertake franchisee of the brand or become a distributor of the company. Similarly, studies have shown that direct selling companies have created significant self-employment opportunities, especially for women, which has led to women empowerment (Mukherjee *et al.*, 2010). However, the employment impact of international businesses is widely debated. Studies (Guruswamy *et al.*, 2005; Sarma, 2005; Singh,

7. *http://www.mcdonaldsindia.net/PressRelease/McDonalds%20india%20(North%20%20East)%20-%20Media%20Fact%20Book_February_2013.pdf* (last accessed on March 4, 2014).
8. Own calculation from *Union Budget 2013-14*. Accessible at *http://indiabudget.nic.in/budget2013-2014/ub2013-14/rec/tr.pdf* and *http://indiabudget.nic.in/ub2006-07/rec/sum.pdf* (last accessed on March 5, 2014).
9. For details see *http://www.nsdcindia.org/pdf/transportation-logistics.pdf* (last accessed on March 18, 2014).
10. *http://dipp.gov.in/English/Discuss_paper/Reponses31_19August2010.pdf* (last accessed on March 3, 2014).
11. *http://www.metro-cc.com/internet/site/mcc/node/323969/Len/index.html*
12. *http://www.csumba.org/mba602/McDonald's%20in%20India.pdf* (last accessed on March 4, 2014).

2010) have shown that international businesses in the retail sector may have a negative impact on traditional retailer outlets and employment loss in the value chain due to elimination of intermediaries. Singh (2011) highlighted that the employment-creating potential of international businesses has been over-estimated. In addition, small retailers in Indian cities like Bangalore have lost income because there has been a high penetration of modern retail. However, there is no formal estimation of actual employment losses in the unorganised sector.

A survey-based study by Mukherjee and Goyal (2012) showed that while there can be debate on employment creation *versus* job losses by foreign retailers compared with traditional outlets, modern retail outlets provide better quality of employment in terms of greater job security, higher compensation and better quality of life for its employees. Employees in modern outlets undergo training that helps in their skill development and improves their job prospects. The study further found that employees in unorganised or traditional food retail sector are willing to work in the modern sector; however, they may not get automatically absorbed in the organised sector as they lack adequate education and skills. Several organised retailers—either individually or through associations such as the Retailer Association of India—have partnered with educational institutes to provide retail-specific training and skill development. Management institutes in India have retail management programmes.

Studies have also shown that international businesses impart training to their contract manufacturers, which helps them become part of the global supply chain (Joseph and Soundararajan, 2009; Mukherjee *et al.*, 2013; Reardon and Gulati, 2008). This also improves their quality consciousness and helps them secure regular clientele. While one segment of society continues to highlight the negative effect of foreign businesses on employment (Guruswamy *et al.*, 2005; Sarma, 2005; Singh, 2010; 2011), if the economy continues to grow, it is likely that the perceived benefits will outnumber the negative effects.

6.4 Creating Backward Linkages

Demand for food products is dominated by local tastes and the preferences of consumers. To a large extent, it also depends on domestic supply and knowledge about the local market. International food businesses, therefore, partner with local players and then set up strong backward linkages by enhanced sourcing of products from the domestic market and bringing better technology in production. Some benefits that can accrue from international businesses are discussed below.

6.4.1 *Sourcing from Farmers, Improving Farm Productivity through Technology Diffusion and Enhanced Income*

The survey found that several international food businesses in India are working with Indian farmers to enhance productivity and the quality of the yield and to provide assured returns to farmers. For instance, Coca-Cola India through project "Unnati" works with farmers and an Indian company to enhance mango yields. Coca-Cola India provides the technology and economical methods of crop irrigation, which are likely to improve farm income (see Box 6.2 for details).

Another example is McCain India Private Limited, a wholly-owned subsidiary of McCain Food Limited, a Canadian company, which has partnered with potato farmers in Gujarat. The company introduced the farmers to modern methods of sowing and reaping crops, resulting in an increase in yield and improved incomes. According to an estimate, in Gujarat McCain India was instrumental in reducing farmers' expenditure by 35 per cent and increased incomes by 104 per cent.[13] The company is not only working towards increasing the potato yield, but also ensuring definite returns to farmers. McCain India supplies to fast food retailers such as McDonald's, thereby ensuring consistent demand for its products. This has opened a new market for potato growers in the state. It has also exposed them to modern techniques of production and developed an understanding of product quality. McDonald's sources its products from Indian suppliers such as Vista Processed Food Private Limited (chicken and vegetables) and Amrit Foods Private Limited (dairy products).[14] Other companies such as PepsiCo India also undertake direct sourcing from India. The company works with potato farmers in Punjab and West Bengal to source raw materials for its brands, such as Frito Lays. It works with around 24,000 farmers across nine states under the collaborative farming model and procures around 45 per cent of its total requirement by working with farmers. The firm assures buyback of the farm produce at pre-agreed prices from cultivators, thus insulating them from market price fluctuations

13. *http://www.mccain.com/GoodPeople/growers/Pages/default.aspx* (last accessed on March 4, 2014).

14. For details, see *http://ojica.fiu.edu/index.php/ojica_journal/article/viewFile/19/18* (last accessed on March 4, 2014).

Box 6.2

Project Unnati: Coca Cola India Private Limited

Coca–Cola India Private Limited, for its mango-based products—Maaza and Minute Maid—is sourcing mangoes from India. Despite being the largest producer of mangoes, India has one of the lowest yields (6 tonnes per hectare) in the world. As a result, India has been losing its dominance in global mango production. In such a situation, Coca-Cola India is trying to build up the mango yield in the country through three ways—Ultra High-Density Plantations (UHDP) in Andhra Pradesh, the Jain Group Irrigation Project and Project Parivartan. Through UHDP, nearly 600 trees instead of only 40 trees can be planted in an acre and mango orchards attain their full potential in 3–4 years.

Figure 6.3

Farming using UHDP

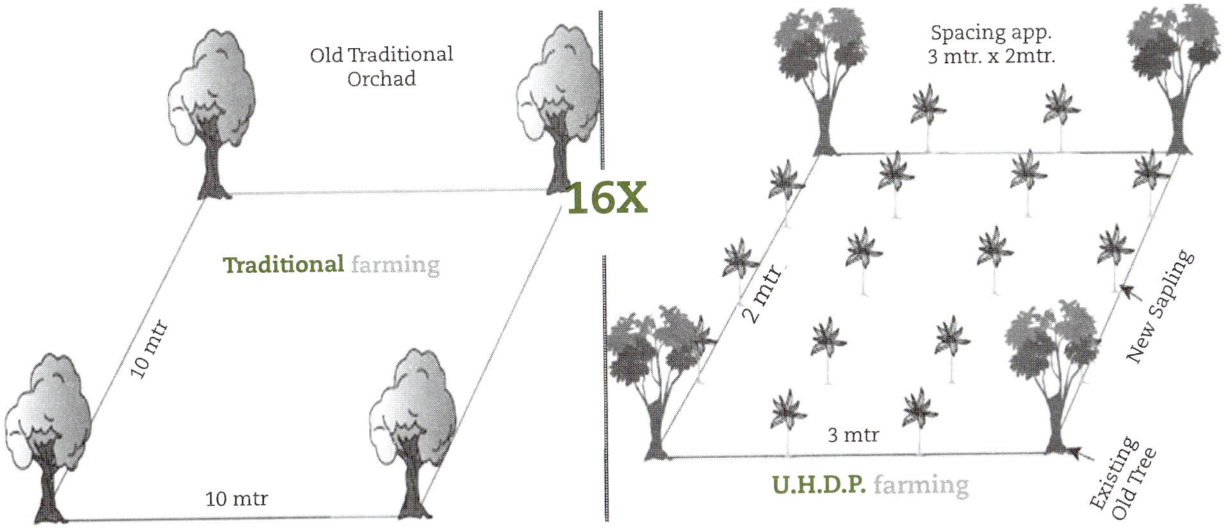

During the first phase of this project, 200 demonstration farms between 1 and 3 acres used the UHDP technique for mango cultivation. In addition, with the help of Jain Irrigation Systems Limited, Coco-Cola India uses drip irrigation, which increases farm income by increasing the yield per acre and simultaneously decreasing the quantity of water used per kilo of mango cultivation. The first phase of the project had an investment outlay of more than $2 million, which will be shared equally by Coca-Cola India and Jain Irrigation Systems Limited. Lastly, Coca-Cola India is training 100,000+ retailers in 2,000+ towns under the Parivartan programme. This includes in-farm practical training, mobile classroom training and visits to demo farms. All this together forms an attempt by Coca-Cola India at improving India's mango production and return to farmers. The Unnati project is likely to target 5,000 farmers in the next five years starting in 2013.

Source: Coca-Cola India Private Limited.

besides ensuring a stable income. PepsiCo India also provides financial support to the farmers by working in a collaborative model with banks and insurance companies; they help farmers obtain collateral-free loans from banks and work with insurance companies for crop insurance.[15]

15. *http://businesstoday.intoday.in/story/pepsico-india-to-scale-up-collaborative-farming/1/198905.html* (last accessed on March 6, 2014) and survey information.

ITC India Private Limited works with Indian farmers through their e-Choupal initiative that uses technology to streamline the supply chain. The company has set up kiosks that are equipped with a computer, internet connectivity through satellite technology and solar power. This provides information about prices, the latest technology, use of seeds and fertilisers and other market and farm-related information. It also provides farmers with a sourcing network that helps improve their margins.

Foreign wholesalers such as Metro Wholesale Cash & Carry India have set up an agricultural sourcing platform in the country. Metro Wholesale Cash & Carry India has 'Farmers' Collection Centres' in five states: Karnataka (Malur), Andhra Pradesh (Vontimamidi), Punjab (Malerkotla), Maharashtra (Manchar) and West Bengal (Barasat).[16] The centres procure fresh fruit and vegetables directly from farmers, who are informed in advance of the requirement so that they can plan their harvest. Metro Cash & Carry not only sources from India for the domestic market but also for its global operations. In 2004, the company entered into an agreement with Punjab Agro Industries Corporation to source food products for its international operations (Mukherjee and Patel, 2005). In addition, the company has opened fish consolidation points in Kameswaram (Tamil Nadu) and Malpe (Karnataka). Carrefour India Private Limited, a subsidiary of Carrefour S.A., procures 90–95 per cent of its products, including grocery, from the Indian market. Carrefour S.A. works with about 90 suppliers/farmers in Uttar Pradesh, Andhra Pradesh, Delhi, Punjab and Haryana, dealing directly with the farmers for quality products.[17]

As most companies are expanding their business in the Indian market, their sourcing from India is likely to increase. Several global retailers such as J Sainsbury Plc and John Lewis Partnership have recently set up sourcing offices in India. Although many of them initially start by sourcing non-food products, with the larger presence of international businesses in India, sourcing from India in food products is expected to increase. It is also important to note that sourcing of global retailers from India is much lower than their sourcing from other countries. For instance, as of 2013, Tesco Plc is sourcing £270 million worth of products from India every year for its global operations compared to a sourcing of £2.25 billion from China.[18] Moreover, due to the lack of supporting regulations (such as contract farming regulations) in certain states farmers can be exploited and paid a lower price by both domestic corporate and foreign companies. However, this can be prevented in a competitive environment, where farmers can select the best price through knowledge sharing and through proper regulations. Moreover, a public private partnership (PPP) can be set up where the government works with farmers and organised players to enable them to become part of the global value chain. For instance, in India, Metro Cash & Carry is working with the Indian government departments and farmers in a PPP model for technological development. Under Project Sheep, Metro along with the Government of Karnataka Sheep and Wool Development Board will train 3,900 farmers in creating quality awareness and will conduct health camps for de-worming and vaccination of sheep.

6.4.2 *Setting up Local Manufacturing and Working with Farmers*

The Indian investment policy is congenial for setting up manufacturing facilities. This has stimulated international businesses to set up manufacturing facilities in the country and create employment and income. The survey found that since Indian consumers are price-conscious, most international brands set up local manufacturing in the country to remain price-competitive and penetrate the Indian market. This has helped boost the manufacturing sector in India. Since manufacturing entails costs and has a long gestation period, once the products penetrate the market and are accepted in the market, foreign companies are more willing to invest in manufacturing.

Setting up manufacturing can boost exports from the country. India is the largest producer of milk and the second largest producer of fruits and vegetables in the world. Thus, India has significant potential to develop as an export hub for raw materials as well as finished products for processed food items (PHD Chamber and Yes Bank, 2012). In recent years, there has been a shift in agricultural production from food grain to high-value agricultural commodities including fruit and vegetables. There is also increased processing of horticultural products such as fruit and vegetables and increased trade in processed fruits and vegetables compared with traditional agricultural commodities (Sharma and Jain, 2011). The increase in exports of fruit and vegetable juices can be attributed to changes in production patterns and the percolation of modern techniques of manufacturing (Mukherjee *et al.*, 2013). For instance, ITC India Private Limited is one of India's largest exporters of agricultural products. The ITC group's contribution to foreign exchange earnings over the past 10 years amounted

16. *http://www.metro-cc.com/internet/site/mcc/node/356793/Len/index.html* (last accessed on March 4, 2014).
17. *http://www.carrefour.in/webapp/wcs/stores/servlet/CPHome?storeId=25051&catalogId=10051&langId=-1#* (last accessed on March 4, 2014).
18. See *http://www.business-standard.com/article/companies/tesco-puts-cash-and-carry-plans-in-india-on-hold-111121200058_1.html* and *http://www.tescoplc.com/index.asp?pageid=290* (last accessed on March 18 2014)

to nearly $5.4 billion, of which agricultural exports constituted 56 per cent.[19]

Nestlé S.A., a Swiss company, opened a milk-processing factory in Moga (Punjab) in 1959. Since then, the supplier base has grown from 4,600 farmers providing 2,000 tonnes of milk to 100,000 farmers in 2,600 villages producing more than 300,000 tonnes. Field camps run by Nestlé Agricultural Services have helped farmers improve their farming practices and milk quality. Separately, the Village Women Development Programme has trained 30,000 women dairy farmers.[20]

Local manufacturing also helps bring in modern technology and environmentally sustainable methods of production. Mukherjee *et al.* (2013) found that large companies (including international businesses) invest in processes such as waste management. According to their survey, around 70 per cent of the corporate manufacturers have invested in R&D activities for product and process development, waste management and water conservation. For instance, PepsiCo India has adopted the 'Waste to Wealth' programme in six municipalities in the states of Tamil Nadu, Andhra Pradesh and Haryana. The programme not only aims to educate the community on recycling waste, but also provides livelihood to more than 600 green ambassador members of the community. As mentioned earlier, companies like Coca-Cola India are collaborating with ventures like Jain Irrigation System Limited in using drip irrigation techniques that help them conserve water.

6.4.3 *Streamlining the Supply Chain*

In India, the supply chain infrastructure is not well developed. As a result, most international companies in food businesses make huge investments in the supply chain, which has led to an improvement in supply chain infrastructure. The survey found that the majority of international businesses have built their own supply chain network or are working closely with foreign logistics service suppliers.

For instance, McDonald's spent six years and around $81.9 million to set up the food supply chain even before opening its first restaurant in the country.[21] It made large investments in infrastructure and supplier development. It has set up a cold-chain to cut down operational wastage and maintain the freshness and nutritional value of raw and processed food products. The cold chain involves procurement, warehousing, transportation and retail of perishable food products—all under controlled temperatures. The McDonald's supply chain begins at the grassroots level, with suppliers receiving the crop directly from farmers. The crop is then processed and despatched to distribution centres in special multi-chamber, temperature-controlled trucks, which ensures that the quality of the supplies is not compromised. The supplies are stored in rooms with different temperature zones and are finally despatched to McDonald's restaurants based on specific demand.[22] One aspect of the supply chain that is crucial to McDonald's is return logistics. For example, the buns are packed in crates and once the buns are unpacked, the crates are return-shipped to the bakeries for use once again.[23] McDonald's uses 8,500–9,000 buns, 3,000–3,500 kilograms of tomatoes, 2,000 kilograms of iceberg lettuce and 5,500 slices of cheese per day. These are delivered to 255 restaurants across India using 60–70 refrigerated trucks. The produce is sourced from 40 different suppliers based across the country.

Companies such as PepsiCo India help reduce losses in transportation and storage by using modern cold stores and transport networks. This reduced losses in transportation from 4 per cent to 1 per cent and storage losses from 9 per cent to 3 per cent. [24]

Companies like Metro Wholesale Cash & Carry and Carrefour India Private Limited have set up their own logistics infrastructure in the country. Carrefour India has also invested in bringing new technology with its infrastructure. For instance, since 2003 the company has adopted Integrated Composite Application Network (ICAN) software to integrate its stores, distribution centres and supply chain partners in various countries. This helps them integrate the supply chain network.

---

19. *http://www.itcportal.com/about-itc/profile/index.aspx* (last accessed on March 6, 2014).
20. *http://www.nestle.com/brands/dairy/dairycsv* (last accessed on March 6, 2014).
21. *http://www.executivetravelmagazine.com/articles/mcdonalds-entry-into-india*
22. *http://www.cio.in/article/mcsupply-top-food-chain*
23. Eating out: A Bite of F&B Food Service in India, Athena Infonomics India Pvt. Ltd.
24. PepsiCo estimates.

Figure 6.4

Transportation and Cold Storage Network used by PepsiCo India

Source: PepsiCo's estimation.

6.5 Creating Forward Linkages: Benefits to the Consumer

International food businesses benefit Indian consumers by providing them with access to a greater variety of products and services at competitive prices. The survey found that as Indian consumers are globalising, the demand for international gourmet products has increased. The demand for imported food products in India has traditionally been for unique products that are not natural to the Indian environment or tastes. For instance, a decade back, pasta and olive oil were not part of the staple Indian diet. However, over time these products are becoming staple food for Indian consumers. The Indian palate is becoming more varied and consumer demands are changing. Imported products and the presence of foreign companies have created a variety of products and widened the choices available to consumers.

International businesses and large retail outlets also provide a good shopping experience for Indian consumers. Companies such as Tesco Plc have adopted integrated service solutions with the help of Indian companies such as Tata Consultancy Services (TCS) to provide a centralised customer care and billing platform.

The survey found that unlike the popular perception, large manufacturers and retailers are now targeting not only higher income consumers but also middle and low-income consumers. This implies that they have to give quality products at low prices and thus consumers are likely to benefit from the presence of organised manufacturers and low-cost volume retailers. For instance, Hindustan Unilever Limited undertakes rural marketing activities to ensure that products reach Indian villages and remote areas through distributors appointed from within the villages (Kaur, 2013). It has introduced value packs for rural customers and extended its reach to cover more than 100,000 villages in India.

With the advent of international businesses, quality consciousness is also rising among Indian consumers. There has been a change in consumption patterns. A study by the Indian Council for Research on International Economic Relations (ICRIER) and the Indian Beverage Association (IBA)[25] found that with the growing economy, increasing incomes, evolving retail structure, wider choice and greater awareness about global and domestic brands, Indian consumers are becoming more knowledgeable. The study found that with the advent of modern retail, 89 per cent of the consumers surveyed reported an increase in quality consciousness. Consumers are also more aware of ingredients and their impacts, manufacturing dates and product packaging.

This discussion shows that the presence of international businesses in the food supply chain has the potential to benefit farmers, manufacturers, consumers and other players in the supply chain.

However, there are two major concerns. The first concern is the possible concentration of market power in the hands of the big players in this sector. In India, farmers are small and fragmented and consequently their ability to bargain is limited. In a traditional supply chain model, farmers often do not receive remunerative prices due to the existence of a large number of intermediaries and inefficiencies in the system. While the entry of big private players, including foreign players, can potentially reduce these inefficiencies, the lack of bargaining power of the farmers does not ensure that the farmers will be able to take advantage of the more efficient supply chain. Unequal bargaining power between the farmers and large private firms implies that the possibility of monopolistic exploitation cannot be ruled out. The policy regime needs to take measures to address this concern. Second, unorganised retail and trading generate large employment in India and there is considerable debate about whether the entry of big private players can displace these people and affect their livelihood. The employment growth rate in India has slowed in the past decade and any major negative impact on employment may create political resistance to the entry of foreign players in the food supply chain in India. The government must ensure that the right policy environment is put in place so that a mutually beneficial and sustainable relationship is established between international business and key players in the food supply chain in India.

25. For details, see Mukherjee *et al.* (2013).

7

Addressing the Policy Gap

This section focuses on policy measures that will enable India to build an efficient food supply chain, enhance FDI inflows, remove wastage and increase the revenue earnings of the government. Over the years, the Indian government has initiated several institutional and regulatory reforms to attract greater private and foreign investment in the food supply chain. However, these should be implemented in a supportive business environment that is investor-friendly and well-governed. The food supply chain in India is regulated by multiple ministries, resulting in multiple and overlapping regulations. Key ministries such as the MOFPI do not have adequate funding. For instance, the government budget for the Ministry of Agriculture for 2012–13 was ₹ 181.73 billion ($3.3 billion) while that for MOFPI was only Rs.6.60 billion ($0.121 billion). The lack of support for the key ministry, which does value addition to agriculture, has been one reason why India has failed to develop as a food processing hub. The budget for MOFPI should at least be doubled. Regulations should be transparent and non-discriminatory and there is a need for greater co-ordination across different government departments. The policy gaps that need immediate attention are discussed below.

7.1 FDI Policy in Multi-brand Retail

One area that requires the immediate attention of the government is the policy of allowing partial FDI in multi-brand retail. The policy is designed to facilitate the entry of global retailers in the food business, but it has failed to attract FDI because it is ambiguous, riddled with conditions and, more recently, some state governments have rolled back the policy. Further, the policy has failed to define retail or understand the different retail formats (store and non-store).

Recently, the government came up with a discussion paper on e-commerce titled "Discussion Paper on E-Commerce in India". This paper lacks clarity on the objective of FDI in e-commerce policy. Before enacting the FDI policy, it is important for policymakers to be clear on its objective.

Ideally, the objective of FDI in the retail policy should be to attract FDI, technology and global best practices, boost consumption and provide access to good quality products for consumers, generate employment (both direct and indirect), enhance manufacturing and improve revenue earnings for the government. The objective of retail regulation is much broader than the FDI policy and it should aim to: (a) create a competitive environment for retailers where there is no discrimination between foreign and domestic large retailers, but certain preferential treatment can be given to small retailers/*kiranas*/ corner shops; (b) regulate anti-competitive practices by addressing issues like predatory pricing and cartelisation in retail; (c) ensure consumer protection; (d) create quality employment and job security; (e) have regulations for zoning, advertising, shop timings, etc.; and (f) incentivise retailers to source from India.

These objectives can be achieved through a simple retail policy. It is important to note that foreign retailers in the food business would like to source from India but often SMEs do not meet their quality standards. Therefore, if the sourcing condition is similar to the policy for single-brand retail where retailers are required to source 'preferably' from micro, small and medium enterprises, it will benefit both the foreign retailer and the country (see Appendix A-2.2 for the single-brand retail policy). It will meet the policy requirement to enhance sourcing from India. Most survey participants were of the view that there should be some sourcing condition and they agreed on the 30 per cent sourcing requirements, but companies should have the freedom to source from whomever they want in India. In fact, the condition of sourcing from SMEs leads to fragmentation in manufacturing and inefficient operations. In the past, India had policies for reservation of certain items for SMEs, which has failed. The government should reconsider the sourcing requirements.

India has a low manufacturing base and a negative balance in trade in goods. One of the concerns of policymakers is that the entry of foreign retailers, who would like to import products through their existing global production network, can worsen India's trade balance. To counter this, there is a need to monitor foreign retailers' performance and sourcing strategy. If the foreign retailer creates employment, is a net foreign exchange earner or is doing more than 80 per cent local sourcing, then the retailer should be encouraged to establish a presence. In fact, in such cases after three years of initial entry the FDI limit can be increased to 75 per cent. This will incentivise the foreign retailer to bring in more investment and to source materials from India.

If there is a zoning regulation, it should cover all large retailers. The FDI policy should not have a condition stating that 'states have the right to decide'. This creates ambiguity. Since foreign venture capitalists are investing in e-commerce, there is no justification to impose specific restrictions in retail formats such as e-commerce.

Foreign retailers have not raised much objection to the minimum capital requirement condition, but they would like the flexibility to decide where they would invest within the food supply chain. The policy should only mention the minimum capital requirement of $100 million and remove the additional clauses that are creating confusion. If the government tries to control where businesses should invest, businesses may decide not to invest at all and this is exactly the case with the present policy on FDI in multi-brand retail.

It is important to note that a brand-based FDI retail policy creates ambiguity in its definition of brands, sub-brands, what products are eligible through the single-brand retail route, etc. The government should open up multi-brand retail in a phased manner, bring uniformity in the single-brand and multi-brand retail policies and within three years remove this brand-based policy. By 2017, there should be one FDI policy for retail as is done by most countries.

7.2 Other Retail Regulations

Retail regulation needs complementary policies. For example, India should strengthen its anti-competitive regulation. The Competition Act, 2002 has provisions to check abuses of their dominant position by major players including predatory pricing. In the Competition Act, dominant position is defined as "a position of strength, enjoyed by an enterprise, in relevant market, in India."[1] However, the dominant position has to be clearly specified in terms of the market size of the retailers, as it is done in Australia. In addition, some countries have specific bodies that regulate competition in the retail sector that may arise due to the dominant position of large retailers. For instance, in the UK there is a Groceries Code Adjudicator that acts as an ombudsman to regulate anti-competitive practices in the retail sector (see Box 7.1). Similar bodies can be established in India to protect smaller players from larger companies.

7.3 Streamline the Sourcing and Supply Chain

There is an urgent need to streamline the food supply chain. Today, India is not a single market for investors in the food business and there are more barriers in moving food products between different states of India than between different member states of the EU. The Indian government has already built the national highways and there is significant investment in state highways. India should now focus on developing dedicated economic corridors. Even if world-class infrastructure is created, there will be delays and wastage due to delays at check-posts and other inter-state barriers. Specifically, India should do away with various entry barriers such as the Way Bill in West Bengal and Octroi in Maharashtra that are levied by different state governments and local bodies, which increase costs and the wait time at check-posts. The speed of traffic movement will increase and wastage will be reduced by replacing the manual check-posts with computerised ones that operate 24x7. There is an urgent need to adopt a single-window clearance system at the check-posts. India can adopt the concept of 'Green Channels' as has been done by the EU Member States; under this system, payments are made online and, by producing the receipt at the check-post, trucks can pass through without queuing to pay toll charges. The concepts of smart cards at check-posts and proper driver's licences would be a pre-requisite. A national register should be developed for all vehicles and traders that frequently use the service. All these will help in faster movement of freight, especially those with a single destination. If adopted, it can considerably reduce wastage of fruits and vegetables and also save time and fuel costs. Currently, this has been adopted by states such as Gujarat (Ministry of Road Transport and Highways, 2011).

In the case of external trade (both exports and imports) the customs processes have to be streamlined and clearance processes should be on the fast track. In this context, India can replicate or emulate global best practices. For instance, New Zealand and Singapore have implemented single-point clearance for all products at the ports. In these countries, any company importing a particular product accesses the country's relevant website and chooses the product from an HS code list at the six-digit level. Accordingly, no-objection certificates, clearances, sample testing, etc., can be done online. The procedures are completed before the product physically reaches the port, which reduces delays and wastage. Computerised risk management systems, as in the EU, reduce the need for physical checks, which saves time. Different authorities clearing consignments should be located in the ports/airports. If a certain product manufactured by a particular company has already cleared the quality standards, it need not be tested each time it is imported and there can be checks at regular intervals.

1. The Competition Act, 2002, No. 12 of 2003. *http://www.unctad.org/sections/ditc_ccpb/docs/ditc_ccpb_ncl_India_en.pdf*

Box 7.1

Groceries Code Adjudicator, Competition Commission

The Groceries Code Adjudicator is the UK's first independent adjudicator to oversee the relationship between supermarkets and their suppliers. It ensures that large supermarkets treat their direct suppliers lawfully and fairly, investigates complaints and arbitrates in disputes. It was constituted in the late nineties and early 2000 to ensure fair trading in the UK. The Code covers only direct suppliers of products who sell through retail outlets in the UK. The office is supported by large retailers, as the majority of the funding comes from them. It aimed to protect small businesses from the larger ones so that large retailers do not push all the competition to suppliers. The Groceries Code Adjudicator adopts the following approach to address an issue related to misuse of dominant position:

- Take a reasonable number of complaints against a retailer.
- Soft approach: Discuss the complaints with the code compliance officer at the company.
- Undertake investigation (9-12 months).
- Issue a recommendation to the retailer.
- Otherwise, publish a statement in the national press.
- Otherwise, fire the faultier.

Source: Primary Survey.

7.4 Fiscal Reforms

There is an urgent need to streamline the multi-layered tax system and implement GST. With proper implementation of GST, manufacturers will be able to locate their processing units in states where the raw materials are available and companies will be able to operate on a hub-and-spoke model. Moreover, manufacturers and retailers can offer a uniform pan-India price. Apart from GST, there should be uniform tax rates across different types of processed food.

7.5 Efficient Implementation of New Regulations

It is important to efficiently implement new regulations. For example, FSSAI does not have the laboratories or manpower to test products and there are significant delays in product approvals. In addition, the FSSAI does not have predefined standards and guidelines for all product categories. This causes delays in obtaining approval and, thereafter, in the establishment of manufacturing facilities. The implementation of regulations varies across different ports of entry and often depends on the individual judgement of the officers present at the port. It is important to note that in most of the cases where imported consignments have been held in ports and products are spoiled, the Indian importers have to bear the losses. There is a need to train officers and create testing laboratories so that the FSSA 2006 is implemented in a smooth manner. Similarly, regulations such as the Legal Metrology Act, 2009, should follow globally accepted procedures and labelling standards. Regulations should not be implemented without prior warning.

7.6 Rationalise Import Duties and Trade Policies

India has one of the highest tariffs for agriculture and the processed food sector. Sometimes, tariffs on raw materials together with the non-availability of local raw materials prompts Indian companies to shift their manufacturing base to other countries. They then use the Indian trade agreements with these countries to import the products duty-free into India. Not only the agro-processing sector in the country and employment suffer due to such tariffs distortions, but the government also faces a revenue loss. The government should examine the import duties and tariff policies, especially with respect to raw material imports. Due to high import duties on packaging materials, agro-products from India such as Basmati rice are packaged in countries such as the United Arab Emirates (UAE) and India is not able to do value addition in the processed food segment.

It is important for Indian policymakers to realise that with globalisation and trade agreements, multinationals and domestic companies are free to relocate to any country with which India has signed a trade agreement and which has a better manufacturing facility and *Ease of Doing Business*. They can then import the product into India. Therefore, India should have a more rational domestic tariff policy and lower tariffs for key imports. It is crucial to have a long-term, predictable, agri-trade policy and a liberalised tariff regime. The trade policy should be equally focused on exports and imports, keeping in mind the requirements of both producers and consumers. Since many raw materials even if they are available in India are not of adequate quality, it is important for the government to impose moderate duties and special exemptions on imports of such products used in manufacturing. During the survey some experts suggested that domestic agriculture prices in India should be based on global agricultural price trends, accounting for both long-term changes and short-term fluctuations. They also highlighted the need to abolish quantitative restrictions or quotas on commodities such as sugar, since these are inefficient and make the trade policy biased.

7.7 Enhance Trust and Collaboration in the Domestic Market through Policy Intervention

The survey highlighted that it is not easy for foreign companies to establish a manufacturing presence in India due to infrastructure and other bottlenecks. They need the support of central and state governments to do businesses. Several multinationals are willing to work with farmers to develop quality raw materials. However, it takes time and such investments have a gestation period. The government, through appropriate policies such as allowing contract farming, can secure the legal rights of both manufacturers and farmers. Similarly, legal contracts will help retailers to establish direct sourcing channels.

7.8 Learn from Global Best Practices

Indian policymakers have to understand the regulations in some key countries and learn from their best practices. The food safety standards, consumer protection regulations and anti-competitive regulations in developed economies such as the EU are more rigid than in India. However, they are also more transparent and uniformly implemented. There is a need for Indian policymakers to understand these best practices.

7.9 Inter-government Collaboration and Information Sharing

Different government departments can collaborate and share information with their counterparts in developed countries to understand how standards are designed and implemented. For example, India can learn from the UK experience of designing policy with respect to FDI in retail, food safety standards, consumer protection regulations and regulating the anti-competitive practices of large retailers, among others. To begin with, an India–UK Joint Committee or a working group can be set up that has representation from different government departments such as MOFPI, FSSAI, the Ministry of Agriculture, the Competition Commission and the Department of Consumer Affairs from India and their counterparts from the UK. This working group should also have representation from key industry associations in India and the UK.

There is a need for the government to provide a platform where businesses can come together to leverage on their mutual strengths and develop products and services for third-country markets. There is a need for government support for joint product promotion events (such as food shows).

If the above reforms are implemented, the distortions in the food supply chain may reduce and India is likely to attract more foreign investment. Manufacturing and organised sector employment may grow. This may also lead to increased sourcing and agro-product exports from India. This will enable the country to develop as an agro-processing hub in the long run.

Conclusion

India, with a large population base, growing per capita income and a large supply of raw materials, can become one of the largest producers and consumers of food. However, the country has not been able to realise its potential. India's food supply chain is fragmented, there are wastages in the supply chain, food inflation is high and the food processing industry, food logistics business and organised food retail are at a nascent stage. The country is facing a slowdown in growth and India is not able to integrate in the global value chain, particularly in the food segment. Despite several government incentives for setting up local manufacturing and imposing high tariffs and other import barriers to protect the domestic industry, organised manufacturing remains small and imports are rising to meet the growing domestic demand. India's negative trade balance is increasing. The country needs foreign and private investments in the food supply chain, but it is not able to attract adequate investments.

Given this background, this report examined the potential for international businesses in the food supply chain in India. Based on a primary survey and secondary information, the report found that international businesses have a significant interest in the Indian market due to the large and growing consumer base as well as for risk diversification. The report found that foreign businesses have responded positively to the liberalisation in FDI. Foreign companies that understood the market dynamics, customised their products to cater to local taste patterns, had the right pricing strategy and changed their business model to meet the market requirements have benefited substantially from their presence in India. The report lists a set of India-specific go-to-market strategies for foreign businesses, highlighting the market complexities and indicating that companies should have a long-term business plan for India with a clearly defined India-specific strategy. Their operating models and strategies in developed countries may not be successful if replicated in India.

The report further highlights that the entry of foreign businesses has benefitted the country. It has created a manufacturing base and employment, generated tax revenue, led to upgrading of skills and technology and higher income for farmers and SME manufacturers, who are gradually becoming a part of the global supply chain of large multinational retailers and manufacturers. Nevertheless, the presence of foreign multinationals in India is far below competing countries such as China, Brazil or Thailand. This is because international businesses face several barriers in India depending on their presence and mode of operation in the food supply chain. Domestic companies also face most of these barriers and, thus, these barriers are related to general ease of doing business in a country. Certain barriers such as restrictions on FDI in multi-brand retail are specific to foreign companies.

The report emphasises that when a country needs foreign investment and technology and would like to strengthen its agro-processing base and create quality jobs in the organised sector, it should have a non-discriminatory and transparent policy environment to support the growth of businesses. The report analyses how the present FDI in retail policy can be made more attractive to foreign investors without compromising on the concerns related to FDI inflows. It lists reform measures that will enable the country to streamline the supply chain. It also emphasises how India can learn from global best practices and how regulatory collaboration with countries such as the UK will benefit India. If the policy reforms listed in this report are implemented, India will not only get the requisite FDI inflows and technology, but would also become part of the global value chains of international businesses.

References

Annamalai, K. and S. Rao (2003). *What Works: ITCs E-Choupal and Profitable Rural Transformation*. World Resource Institute and University of Michigan.

ASSOCHAM and Yes Bank (2012). *FDI in Retail: Advantage Farmers*, Food and Agribusiness. New Delhi: Strategic Advisory and Research, Yes Bank. *http://www.assocham.org/arb/general/Background-FDI-Retail.pdf* (last accessed on March 11, 2014).

Deloitte-ICC (2012). *Logistics Sector: Present Situation and Way Forward*. Deloitte Touche Tohmatsu India Private Limited. *http://www.deloitte.com/assets/Dcom-India/Local%20Assets/Documents/Thoughtware/Logistics%20Sector-Present%20situation%20and%20way%20forward.pdf* (last accessed on March 11, 2014).

Ernst and Young (2012). *Ready for the Transition: Ernst and Young's 2012 Attractiveness Survey India*. EYGM Limited. India. *http://emergingmarkets.ey.com/wp-content/uploads/downloads/2012/03/india-attractiveness-final-version1.pdf* (last accessed on March 11, 2014).

Guruswamy, M., K. Sharma, J.P. Mohanty and T.J. Korah (2005). "FDI in India's Retail Sector: More Bad than Good?", *Economic and Political Weekly* 40(7): 619-62.

Images (2009). *India Retail Report 2009*. New Delhi: Images Group.

IMF (2012). *World Economic Outlook: Coping with High Debt and Sluggish Growth*. Washington, D.C.: International Monetary Fund.

Joseph, M. and N. Soundararajan (2009). *Retailing in India: A Critical Assessment*. New Delhi: Academic Foundation.

Joshi, K. (2009). *Processed Food and Beverage Industry: An Overview—S&T and Industry*. New Delhi: National Institute of Science Technology and Development Studies.

Kaur, M. (2013). "Rural Marketing: A Case Study on Hindustan Unilever Limited", *International Journal of Applied Research and Studies* 2(6): 1-14.

KPMG (2013). *Collaborating for Growth: Report on Franchising Industry in India 2013*. India. *http://www.kpmg.com/IN/en/IssuesAndInsights/ArticlesPublications/Documents/Collaborating_for_Growth.pdf* (accessed on February 19, 2014)

McKinsey Global Institute (2007). *The Bird of Gold: The Rise of India's Consumer Market*. McKinsey & Company, India. *http://www.mckinsey.com/insights/asia-pacific/the_bird_of_gold* (last accessed on March 14, 2014).

Mukherjee, A. and N. Patel (2005). *FDI in Retail Sector: India*. New Delhi: Academic Foundation.

Mukherjee, A., D. Mukherjee, D. Ghosh and D. Satija (2013). *Food Processing Industry in India: Unleashing the Potential of the Non-alcoholic Beverage Sector*. New Delhi: Academic Foundation.

Mukherjee, A., D. Satija, T.M. Goyal, M.K. Mantrala and S. Zou (2012). "Are Indian Consumers Brand Conscious? Insights for Global Retailers", *Asia Pacific Journal of Marketing and Logistics* 24(3): 482-99.

Mukherjee, A., T.M. Goyal, D. Satija and N. Soundararajan (2010). *Socio-Economic Impact of Direct Selling: Need for Policy Stimulus*. New Delhi: ICRIER.

Mukherjee, A. and T.M. Goyal (2012). "Employment Conditions in Organised and Unorganized Retail: Implications for FDI Policy in India", *Journal of Business and Retail Management Research* 6(2): 26-37.

National Commission on Population (2006). *Population Projections for India and States 2001-2026: Report of the Technical Group on Population Projections Constituted by the National Commission on Population*. New Delhi: Office of Registrar General and Census Commissioner. *http://www.jsk.gov.in/projection_report_december2006.pdf* (last accessed on March 11, 2014).

Pachouri, A. (2013). "Poor Farm-Market Linkages in India's Agriculture Value Chains", *Farmers Forum* 13(1): 55-56.

PHD Chambers of Commerce and Industry and Yes Bank Limited (2012). *India's Cold Chain Sector: A Diagnostic and Prescriptive Study*. New Delhi: Food and Agribusiness Strategic Advisory and Research (FASAR), Yes Bank Limited.

Rao, S.L. (2000). "India's Rapidly Changing Consumer Markets", *Economic and Political Weekly* 35(40): 3570-72.

Reardon, T. and A. Gulati (2008). "The Supermarket Revolution in Developing Countries: Policies for Competitiveness with Inclusiveness", *IFPRI Policy Brief*. New Delhi: International Food Policy Research Institute.

Reardon, T. and B. Minten (2011). "The Quiet Revolution in India's Food Supply Chain", *IFPRI Discussion Paper* 01115. New Delhi: International Food Policy Research Institute.

Sarma, E.A.S (2005). "Need for Caution in Retail FDI", *Economic and Political Weekly* 40(46): 4795-98.

Sharma, K. (2013). "A Case-Study on McDonald's Supply-Chain in India", *Asia Pacific Journal of Marketing & Management Review* 2(1): 112-20.

Sharma, V.P. and D. Jain (2011). "High-Value Agriculture in India: Past Trends and Future Prospects", *Indian Institute of Management Ahmedabad Working Paper* No. 2011-07-02. *http://www.iimahd.ernet.in/assets/upload/faculty/678631189High%20Value%20Agri.%20Working%20Paper.pdf* (last accessed on March 12, 2014).

Shukla, R. (2010). *How India Earns, Spends and Saves: Unmasking the Real India*. New Delhi: Sage Publications and NCAER.

Singh, S. (2010). "Implications of FDI in Food Supermarkets", *Economic and Political Weekly* 45(34): 17-20.

———. (2011). "FDI in Retail: Misplaced Expectations and Half-truth", *Economic and Political Weekly* XLVI(51): 13-16

Sinha, P.K. and S.K. Kar (2007). "An Insight into the Growth of New Retail Formats in India", *Indian Institute of Management Ahmedabad Working Paper* No. 2007-03-04. *http://iimahd.ernet.in/assets/snippets/workingpaperpdf/2007-03-04_PKSinha.pdf* (last accessed in June 2013).

The Boston Consulting Group (2012). *The Tiger Roars: An In-depth Analysis of How a Billion Plus People Consume*. The Boston Consulting Group, India. *http://www.indiaretailing.com/upload/ContentImage/Market_Research_pdf/The_Tiger_Roars.pdf* (last accessed in July 2013).

WTO (2012). *World Tariff Profiles: 2012*. Geneva: World Trade Organization. Accessible at *http://www.wto.org/english/res_e/booksp_e/tariff_profiles12_e.pdf* (last accessed on March 10, 2014).

Appendix

A-2.1

Licences Required in the Retail Sector

Issuing Authority	*Licence/Permission*
Local Municipal Corporation	Shops and Establishments Trade Licences Food handlers certificate Licence for frozen non-vegetarian food Freezers/chillers 390 permit Sky Signs: licence for hoarding & display windows (permission code) Licence for conducting business of warehouseman in the warehouse subject to the provision of the local Warehouse Act Municipality Licences (local clearance) Valet parking Storage of yarn / inflammable goods
Drug Inspector of Food & Drug Department	Homeopathic Licence Licence for sale of cosmetics under Drugs and Cosmetics Act Restricted Drug Licence under Drugs and Cosmetics Act
Regional FSSAI Office	Food Safety and Standards Act AGMARK Licence under provisions of The Agricultural Produce (Grading and Marking) Act, 1937 Restaurant Grade Licence
Labour Commissioner	Labour licence/7 days working permission Working in shifts
Senior Inspector of Licence Department of Municipal Corporation	Licence issued by the Licence Department, Municipal Corporation, permitting use of illuminated show cases Licence issued by Municipal Corporation, permitting the use of sewing machines
Local Food Commissioner	Milk and Milk Products Order
Local Labour Commissioner	Contract Labour Registration Contract Labour Licence
Local Legal Metrology	Standard of Weights and Measurements Act—Repacking, etc. Standard of Weights and Measurements Act—Measurement calibration and certification
Local Police Station	Police Clearance
Local Police Commissioner	Police Commissioner Permission Police Permission for Eatery
Ministry of Health, Health Department, Municipal Corporation	Food licence to store food products from the Medical Officer of Health of Municipal Corporation Licence to operate a staff canteen inside the establishment FSSAI licence

Contd...

...contd...

Regional Transport Office	Traffic Police NOC Motor Vehicle Act
National / State ESIC Commissioner	ESIC Sub-Code
Local *Gram Panchayat*	Grampanchayat N.O.C
Sub-Controller of Food & Supply	Baby Food Licence
Local Agriculture Department	Insecticide Licence
Regional Excise Commissioner	Beer & Wine
Local Fire Station	Fire Service Station
State APMC	Clearance under Agriculture Produce Marketing Committee Act
State Civil Supply Department / Director	Civil Supply Licence
National Phonographic Performance Ltd.	Phonographic Performance Ltd. (for playing music)
ESIC Department	Certificate of Registration issued under the Employees State Insurance Act, 1948, for stores
Electrical Inspector of public works division	Permission from state electricity board/municipal authorities/government for use of generators/D.G. sets
State Pollution Control Board	Environment-related approvals including consents from pollution control boards that any of the stores of the company might require
Lift Inspector	Licence and registration to work a lift/escalator under applicable state rules
Controller of Rationing	Licence under Essential Commodities Act, 1955
Labour Department	Licence issued by Assistant Inspector of Labour under Festival Holiday Rules
Senior Inspector of Shops Department	Shops and Establishments Certificate
National Indian Performing Rights Society	Indian Performing Rights Society
Regional Municipal Corporation	Food product order/meat products order

Source: Information received during the survey.

A-2.2

Retail FDI Conditions as of August 2013

1. Conditions on Single-brand Retail

- ***Definition:***
  - Products to be sold should be of a 'single-brand' only.
  - Products should be sold under the same brand internationally i.e., products should be sold under the same brand in one or more countries other than India.
  - 'Single-brand' product-retail trading would cover only products which are branded during manufacturing.
  - Only one non-resident entity, whether owner of the brand or otherwise, shall be permitted to undertake single-brand product retail trading in the country, for the specific brand, directly or through a legally tenable agreement, with the brand owner for undertaking single-brand product retail trading. The onus for ensuring compliance with this condition will rest with the Indian entity carrying out single-brand product retail trading in India. The investing entity shall provide evidence to this effect at the time of seeking approval, including a copy of the licensing/franchise/sub-licence agreement, specifically indicating compliance with the above condition. The requisite evidence should be filed with the Reserve Bank of India (RBI) for automatic route and Secretariat for Industrial Assistance (SIA)/Foreign Investment Promotion Board (FIPB) for cases involving approval.
- ***Other Conditions:***
  - In respect of proposals involving foreign direct investment (FDI) beyond 51 per cent, sourcing of 30 per cent of the value of goods purchased will be done from India, preferably from micro, small and medium enterprises (MSMEs), village and cottage industries, artisans and craftsmen, in all sectors. The quantum of domestic sourcing will be self-certified by the company, to be subsequently checked, by statutory auditors, from the duly certified accounts which the company will be required to maintain. This procurement requirement would have to be met, in the first instance as an average of five years total value of the goods purchased, beginning 1st April of the year during which the first tranche of FDI is received. Thereafter, it would have to be met on an annual basis. For the purpose of ascertaining the sourcing requirement, the relevant entity would be the company, incorporated in India, which is the recipient of FDI for the purpose of carrying out single-brand product retail trading.
  - Retail trading, in any form, by means of e-commerce, would not be permissible for companies with FDI, engaged in activities of single-brand retail trading.

2. Conditions on Multi-brand Retail

- *Minimum Capital Requirement:* Minimum amount to be brought in, as FDI, by the foreign investor, would be $100 million.
- *Requirement of Back-end Investments*: At least 50 per cent of total FDI brought in the first tranche of $100 million should be invested in 'back-end infrastructure' within three years, where back-end infrastructure will include capital expenditure on all activities, excluding that on front-end units; for instance, back-end infrastructure will include investment made towards processing, manufacturing, distribution, design improvement, quality control, packaging, logistics, storage, warehouse, agriculture market produce infrastructure, etc. Expenditure on land cost and rentals, if any, will not be counted for purposes of back-end infrastructure. Subsequent investment in back-end infrastructure would be made by the multi-brand retailer as needed, depending upon its business requirements.
- *Sourcing Condition*: At least 30 per cent of the value of procurement of manufactured/processed products purchased should be sourced from Indian MSMEs, which have a total investment in plant and machinery not exceeding $2.00 million. This valuation refers to the value at the time of installation, without providing for depreciation. The 'small industry' status would be reckoned only at the time of first engagement with the retailer and such industry shall continue to qualify as a 'small industry' for this purpose even if it outgrows the said investment of $2.00 million, during the course of its relationship with the said retailer. Sourcing from agricultural cooperatives and farmer cooperatives would be considered in this category. The procurement requirement would have to be met, in the first instance, as an average of five

years total value of the manufactured/ processed products purchased, beginning 1st April of the year during which the first tranche of FDI is received. Thereafter, it would have to be met on an annual basis. Companies have to provide self-certification regarding their MSME status, which could be cross-checked, as and when required. Accordingly, the investors should maintain accounts, duly certified by statutory auditors.

- *Zoning Requirement:* Retail sales outlets may be set up only in cities with a population of more than 10 lakh as per 2011 Census or any other cities as per the decision of the respective state government and may also cover an area of 10 kms around the municipal/urban agglomeration limits of such cities; retail locations will be restricted to conforming areas as per the master/zonal plans of the concerned cities and provision will be made for requisite facilities such as transport connectivity and parking.
- *Procurement Condition:* Government will have the first right to procurement of agricultural products.
- *States have the Right to decide whether or not to allow FDI:* Policy is an enabling policy only and the state governments/union territories would be free to take their own decisions in regard to implementation of the policy. Therefore, retail sales outlets may be set up in states/union territories that have agreed, or agree in future, to allow FDI in multi-brand retail under this policy. The list of states/union territories which have conveyed includes Andhra Pradesh, Assam, Delhi, Haryana, Himachal Pradesh, Jammu & Kashmir, Karnataka, Maharashtra, Manipur, Rajasthan, Uttarakhand, and Daman & Diu and Dadra and Nagar Haveli (union territories). The establishment of the retail sales outlets will be in compliance of applicable state/union territory laws/regulations, such as the Shops and Establishments Act.
- *E-commerce Restriction:* Retail trading, in any form, by means of e-commerce, would not be permissible, for companies with FDI, engaged in the activity of multi-brand retail trading.

A-2.3

Selected Acts and Regulations Related to Production, Distribution and Retail of Food Products

Act/Regulation	*Regulatory authority*	*Production Stage*	*Processing Stage (packaging and labelling)*	*Distribution Stage*	*Retail Stage*	*Import*	*Voluntary/ mandatory implementation at state level*
Food Safety Standards Act, 2006	Ministry of Health and Family Welfare	✓	✓	✓	✓	✓	Mandatory
Agriculture Produce and Voluntary	State governments Marketing Committee Act (reformed in June 2008)			✓			Voluntary
Essential Commodities Act, 1955	State governments/ Union Territories	✓		✓			Mandatory
Drugs and Cosmetics Act, 1940	Ministry of Health and Family Welfare				✓	✓	Mandatory
The Warehousing (Development and Regulation) Act, 2007	Ministry of Consumer Affairs, Food & Public Distribution			✓			Mandatory
Warehousing Corporation Act, 1962				✓			
Shops and Establishments Act, 1953	State governments				✓		Mandatory
Grading and Marketing Act, 1937	Directorate of Marketing and Inspection (DMI) under Ministry of Agriculture		✓				Voluntary
Bureau of Indian Standards' Voluntary (BIS), 1987 Regulations	Ministry of Consumer Affairs, Food & Public Distribution	✓	✓				Voluntary
Export Quality Control Inspection Act, 1963	Export Inspection Council (EIC), Ministry of Commerce	✓	✓				Mandatory
Legal Metrology Act, 2009	State government, Directorate of Weights and Measures under the Ministry of Food and Civil Supplies	✓	✓	✓			Mandatory
Plant Quarantine (Regulation of Import into India) Order, 2003 and amendment	Ministry of Agriculture					✓	Mandatory
Livestock Importation Act, 1898	Ministry of Agriculture					✓	Mandatory
Agricultural and Processed Food Products Export Cess Act, 1985	Ministry of Food Processing Industries and Ministry of Agriculture					✓	Mandatory
Agricultural Produce Cess Act, 1940	Ministry of Food Processing Industries and Ministry of Agriculture					✓	Mandatory
SEZ Act, 2005	Ministry of Commerce and Industry	✓					Mandatory
Land Acquisition Act, 1894	Ministry of Rural Development	✓					Mandatory

Source: Government of India websites.